ESSENTIALS OF IRI

With my very best
wishes

Mary

ESSENTIALS
OF IRISH
LABOUR
LAW

Mary Faulkner

GILL & MACMILLAN

Gill & Macmillan Ltd
Hume Avenue
Park West
Dublin 12
with associated companies throughout the world
www.gillmacmillan.ie

978 07171 40183

Index compiled by Cover to Cover
Print origination in Ireland by TypeIT, Dublin

The paper used in this book is made from the wood pulp of
managed forests. For every tree felled, at least one tree is
planted, thereby renewing natural resources.

A CIP catalogue record for this book is available
from the British Library.

ACKNOWLEDGMENTS

There are a number of people I wish to acknowledge who assisted in the writing of this book. Foremost among them is my family whose support and unstinting patience was invaluable. I also wish to thank my friends for their support and encouragement. A significant debt of gratitude is owed to two of my colleagues, Roderick Maguire, BL and Marian Jennings, Solicitor and Law Lecturer who cast an expert eye over parts of the text at critical moments. I have endeavoured to state the law as of 31 October 2007.

To

Colman, Emmet and Fearghal

CONTENTS

ABBREVIATIONS

CC	Circuit Court
CEEP	European Centre of Enterprise with Public Participaton
CSO	Central Statistics Office
EA	Equality Authority
EAT	Employment Appeals Tribunal
EC	European Community
ECJ	European Court of Justice
EEA	European Economic Area
ESRI	Economic and Social Research Institute
ETUC	European Trade Union Confederation
EU	European Union
GNP	Gross National Product
HSA	Health and Safety Authority
HC	High Court
IBEC	Irish Business and Employers Confederation
ICTU	Irish Congress of Trade Unions
IRO	Industrial Relations Officer
LRC	Labour Relations Commission
PIAB	Personal Injuries Assessment Board
SC	Supreme Court
UNICE	Union of Industrial and Employers' Confederation of Europe

chapter 1

SOURCES

> This chapter will examine the main sources of law that apply in the area of employment. It will also consider contracts of employment and the definition of an employee.
>
> The main sources of employment law in Ireland are:
> 1. Legislation.
> 2. EU law.
> 3. Common law.
> 4. The Constitution.
> 5. Employment Contracts.

1 Legislation

Legislation, which is also known as statutory law or enacted law, is law that has been promulgated or enacted by a legislature. In Ireland that legislature is known as the Oireachtas. The Oireachtas comprises the President (an tUachtaráin) and two Houses: Dáil Éireann (House of Representatives) and Seanad Éireann (the Senate). Before a piece of legislation becomes law it is known as a Bill.

Legislation may be categorised as **superior legislation** and **delegated legislation**.

Superior Legislation

Article 15(2)(1) of the Constitution states that:

> The sole and exclusive power of making laws for the State is hereby vested in the Oireachtas: no other legislative authority has power to make laws for the State.

This Article must be read in conjunction with Art 29(4)(v), on International Relations:

> No provision of this Constitution invalidates laws enacted, acts done or measures adopted by the State which are necessitated by the obligations of membership of the European Union or of the Communities, or prevents laws enacted, acts done or measures adopted by the European Union or by the Communities or by institutions thereof, or by bodies competent under the Treaties establishing the Communities, from having the force of law in this State.

Legislation is first presented as a Bill and then proceeds through five stages in the Oireachtas before being referred to the President to be signed into law. Generally, Bills may be introduced in either the Seanad or in the Dáil, with the exception of Money Bills, Bills to amend the Constitution (Dáil only) and Private Bills (Seanad only).

The first stage is, therefore, the presentation of the Bill. The second stage is the examination of the Bill by the whole House. The third stage is the committee stage, during which a detailed examination of the Bill is carried out by the whole House and by a select committee or by a special committee. The fourth stage is the review stage, when changes made at the third stage are reviewed. The fifth stage is the final stage, when a debate takes place on the motion, '*That this Bill do now pass*'. If passed, the Bill is then sent to the other House, where a similar process is followed. When the Bill has passed through all stages it is presented to the President, who signs it into law. If, having consulted with the Council of State, the President believes the Bill, or part thereof, to be repugnant to the Constitution, it may be passed to the Supreme Court for a decision on its constitutionality, under Art 26. A Bill so referred and declared to be constitutional may not be the subject of a legal challenge again. *In the matter of Article 26 and in the Matter of the Employment Equality Bill 1996* is an example of just such a reference. In this case, which was heard in 1997, the Supreme Court held that a number of the proposed provisions were repugnant to the Constitution, principally those concerning disability and vicarious liability. The Bill was enacted in 1998. As it was the subject of an Art 26 referral, it is now immune to any further constitutional challenge.

Delegated Legislation
Delegated legislation is subordinate legislation made by bodies given power to do so under an Act and arises from parent legislation enacted by the Oireachtas. Power to make subordinate law is delegated to a Minister or a local authority or other competent body to legislate for specific purposes. This type of legislation may take a variety of forms, including Ministerial orders, by-laws and rules of professional bodies. The Safety, Health and Welfare at Work (General Applications) Regulations 2007, introduced by means of a Statutory Instrument, is one example of delegated legislation.

2 EU Law
One source of employment law that has become increasingly important in recent years is European law. This is evident in the fact that much of the employment legislation that has been enacted in Ireland in the last number of years has been driven by developments within European law.

When Ireland became a member of the European Community (as it then was) in 1973, powers had to be devolved to an external body to make laws that would have effect in the State. As the 1937 Constitution placed that role exclusively within the power of the Oireachtas, an amendment to the Constitution was necessary to facilitate this change. In a referendum in 1972 the people passed the Third Amendment to the Constitution, thus paving the way for the European Communities Act 1972 (as amended) to give effect to the constitutional amendment.

The primary law of the European Union (EU) is to be found in the Treaties setting up the various communities, i.e.:

- the Treaty of Paris 1951, which established the European Coal and Steel Community (ECSC);
- the Treaty of Rome 1957, which established the European Economic Community (EEC) and the European Atomic Energy Community (Euratom);
- the Single European Act 1986;
- the Maastricht Treaty on European Union 1992;
- the Treaty of Amsterdam 1997;
- the Treaty of Nice 2001.

As the Constitution of Ireland is supreme, in order for any Treaty to have legal effect in this State a referendum must be held to amend the Constitution.

Secondary law of the EU comprises Directives and Regulations. Directives are given effect by domestic legislation passed for that purpose. Generally, Member States have until a particular date to implement a Directive. Directive 99/70/EC and the implementing piece of legislation, the Protection of Employees (Fixed-Term Work) Act 2003, illustrate the difficulties that arose out of the Government's failure to implement by 10 July 2001, as required. A swathe of litigation followed this failure, with litigants relying on the Directive itself by using the doctrine of direct effect.

Regulations, on the other hand, do not require any intervening step, are applicable directly and are binding in their entirety. They have the purpose and effect of securing uniformity of law.

Another important source of European law concerns decisions of the European Court of Justice (ECJ), which are binding in Irish law.

European Union law takes precedence over Irish domestic law. Article 29, as amended, provides for this.

3 Common Law

Common law is judge-made law. It consists of decisions, particularly those of the superior courts, arising out of cases that come before the courts. In Ireland the superior courts are the High Court and the Supreme Court. A decision in a case is determined by decisions reached in previous cases and the decision thus taken will operate to affect the law to be applied in similar and subsequent cases. Where there is no authoritative statement on the issue in question, the judges have the authority to create law or to establish a precedent. The new decision will bind future courts under the principle of *stare decisis*. Decisions from the superior courts in other jurisdictions may be cited in an Irish court, but will have persuasive authority only. In addition to deciding cases, the courts have the important role of interpreting legislation.

Common law is so called because it was *common* to a number of jurisdictions, particularly those with an historical association with Britain—an association that was not always welcome. The common law formed the basis of the legal systems of England and Wales (though not of Scotland), of Northern Ireland, the Republic of Ireland and the USA (except Louisiana), of Canada (except Quebec) and of Nicaragua, Australia, New Zealand, South Africa, India, Pakistan, Malaysia, Brunei, Singapore and Hong Kong.

Scotland has a legal system that is quite distinct from that which operates in England, Wales and Northern Ireland and owes its development to a number of influences. It is not an original legal system. The main influences contributing to the development of Scottish law include feudal law (landownership), canon law (marriage and succession), Roman law (contracts), English law (statute law, doctrine of judicial precedent), statute law or legislation passed by parliament.

Before common law gained ground in Ireland there was an original legal system in place known as Brehon law, which has been acknowledged as a very sophisticated system. Deriving its name from the Gaelic term for judge, *breitheamh*, it existed for centuries, often in parallel and/or in conflict with either canon law or common law. Brehon law was a secular and original system of Irish civil law, with precise rules set down for the management of society and its relations with the world, both commercial and personal. The law was produced by the judges (*breitheamh*) and could be found in a number of law tracts written in Old Irish, the largest being the *Senchas Mor,* consisting of forty-seven tracts. The *Book of Acaill* set out the law on tort and injuries.

The rules forming the substantive law of the period provide a useful window into the mores and way of life of early Irish society. Rules set down in these law tracts covered all aspects of life, such as marriage, succession, property ownership, copyright, contracts, negligence, fraud, drunkenness, third-party guarantees, hostage-taking, satire and much more. Seemingly modern issues, such as sexual harassment and verbal assault, were also recognised in Brehon law, with penalties and fines being imposed on the perpetrator. There are numerous other hints of a more modern Irish legal system. *Unjustified satire* was prohibited and not only attracted a fine but the wrongdoer also had to make a public retraction. Contracts had a cooling-off period, allowing either party to cancel before sunset. Compensation was the favoured penalty imposed for infringements rather than death or mutilation, which were commonly applied in other early legal systems of the time.

Though early Irish society was male-dominated, women had greater freedom and rights to property than in other contemporary European societies. Divorce existed, with grounds for successful petition including impotence, revealing secrets of the marriage and the non-disclosure by a husband that he was a priest, to name but a few. In a divorce situation property could not be disposed of without the consent of both spouses.

Though under pressure from a foreign system of law introduced in 1169 by the Norman invaders, it was not until the end of the sixteenth century, and particularly with the Flight of the Earls to mainland Europe in 1607, that the Brehon system truly came to an end.

4 The Constitution

The most important source of Irish law is the Constitution or Bunreacht na hÉireann 1937, known as 'de Valera's Constitution'. It is the most important source in that it is superior to all other types of law and no laws may be passed in the State that infringe upon any of its provisions.

There are few direct references to labour law issues in the Constitution. What references there are can be found in the following Articles:

Article 40.1

> All citizens shall, as human persons, be held equal before the law. This shall not be held to mean that the State shall not in its enactments have due regard to differences of capacity, physical and moral, and of social function.

Article 40.6

> The State guarantees liberty for the exercise of the following rights, subject to public order and morality -
> (iii) The right of the citizens to form associations and unions.

Article 45.2.1

> That the citizens (all of whom, men and women equally, have the right to an adequate means of livelihood) may through their occupations find the means of making reasonable provision for their domestic needs.

Article 45.4.2

> The State shall endeavour to ensure that the strength and health of workers, men and women, and the tender age of children shall

not be abused and that citizens shall not be forced by economic necessity to enter avocations unsuited to their sex, age and strength.

More controversial, but clearly a product of its time, is Art 41.2.1 on women in the home, which states:

The State shall, therefore, endeavour to ensure that mothers shall not be obliged by economic necessity to engage in labour to the neglect of their duties in the home.

While there are few references to labour law issues in the Constitution, it is to the unenumerated rights that one must look to appreciate the considerable contribution the Constitution has made to the development of labour law. Unenumerated rights are those rights that have been implied by the Constitution. According to O'Dalaigh J., upholding the views of Kenny J. in *Ryan v Attorney General* [1965] SC, a case concerning the fluoridation of water:

… personal rights mentioned in S 3.1 are not exhausted by the enumeration of life, person, good name and property rights.

This landmark case established the existence of *unenumerated* personal rights contained in Art 40.3 of the Constitution. In the same case, Kenny J. held that:

… there are many personal rights of the citizen which follow from the Christian and democratic nature of the State which are not mentioned in Article 40 at all – the right to free movement within the state and the right to marry are examples of this. This also leads to the conclusion that the general guarantee extends to rights not specified in Article 40.

Since that case a wealth of implied personal rights have been established, including the right to marital privacy (*McGee v Attorney General* [1974]), the right to earn a livelihood (*Murtagh Properties v Cleary* [1972]), the right to fair procedures (*State (Healy) v Donoghue* [1976]) and the right to fair procedures in the decision-making process affecting an individual (*Gleeson v Minister for Defence* [1976]), to name but a few. Many of the fundamental human rights we enjoy today originated under Art 40.3.

Article 40.3.1 provides that:

The State guarantees in its laws to respect, and as far as practicable, by its laws to defend and vindicate the personal rights of the citizen.

In *Murtagh Properties v Cleary* [1972] IR 330 the plaintiff publicans sought an injunction to prevent the picketing of their premises by a trade union, the National Union of Vintners, Grocers and Allied Trades Assistants. The union had objected to the employment of female staff as part-time bar waitresses and argued that such employment was in breach of an agreement between the union and an employers' association. The plaintiffs argued that there was a constitutional right to earn a living without discrimination on the grounds of sex. That right was being infringed, it was contended, when an employer was prevented from employing a person solely on the grounds of gender. Article 45.2.1 (see above) was referred to by the court and for the first time it was recognised that this Article could give rise to a decision on whether an alleged constitutional right existed or not. Kenny J. noted that, regarding the right to an adequate means of livelihood, men and women were to be treated equally. It followed that where an employer was being prevented from employing men or women on the ground of gender, this was contrary to the Constitution.

Another area that has benefited from the provisions of the Constitution relates to fair procedures and natural justice, which are of particular importance in relation to disciplinary procedures in a workplace. In *Garvey v Ireland* [1980] IR 75 the Commissioner of An Garda Síochána had his dismissal declared invalid because of the absence of fair procedures. As he had not been afforded the opportunity to make any representations before his removal from office, he had thus been denied fundamental rights guaranteed under the Constitution.

5 Employment Contracts

An employment contract does not differ from contracts in any other context; the same rules and principles apply. A contract may be defined as an agreement between two parties that creates legally enforceable obligations. As with any other contract, a contract of employment will comprise the essential elements of an offer, an acceptance, consideration and the intention to create legal relations. It may be expressed or implied, oral or in writing.

While there is no obligation for an employment contract to be in writing, certain Acts require that particular terms must be provided in writing to an employee within two months of commencing employment. In the interests of certainty, it is advisable that the terms and conditions are in written form and signed by both parties as evidence of the existence of the contract and those terms.

The terms included in an employment contract or written statement should refer to the following:
- the names of the parties, the employer and employee;
- the place or places of work (may include a mobility clause);
- job title or job description;
- commencement date;

- probationary period;
- where applicable, the duration of a temporary or fixed-term contract and the objective condition determining the fixed-term contract;
- remuneration and method of calculation, payment intervals—whether a week, a month or other interval;
- bonus payments, details of expenses;
- deductions from pay;
- hours of work;
- leave;
- sick leave, notification requirements and whether such leave is paid;
- disciplinary and grievance procedures;
- policies on bullying and harassment;
- email, internet and telephone usage;
- if appropriate, a restraint of trade or confidentiality clause;
- details in respect of possible changes to the contract;
- normal retirement age;
- notice period on resignation or termination;
- health, safety and welfare.

In addition to the above terms expressed in a contract or statement of employment, terms described as implied terms will also govern the contract. These implied terms will most commonly operate by virtue of certain legislation, but may also originate in the common law. Examples of such terms include the duty to follow reasonable orders, to act with honesty and loyalty, not to act contrary to an employer's interest, to pay wages and the duty of mutual trust and confidence in the employment relationship (see below, *Berber v Dunnes Stores* HC 2007). The right to equal pay for like work is implied into all contracts by virtue of the Employment Equality Acts.

In addition to contracts of employment, handbooks should be provided to employees setting out the policies and procedures that apply in the workplace. This is of particular relevance in relation to issues of disciplinary action, health and safety and policies in respect of bullying and harassment. Such handbooks should be reviewed regularly and updated as appropriate.

• Definition of 'Employee'

Employees are generally persons engaged under a contract of employment (or a contract of service) with an employer. There are slight variations of this description in the Acts governing employment. The central issue is whether a person is employed under a **contract of service** or under a **contract for services.** A person working under a **contract of service** is an employee and is covered and protected by employment laws. A person operating under a **contract for services** is a self-employed contractor and is generally not protected by such legislation. There are many instances where it may be difficult to differentiate between the two, and an examination of what the person actually does is necessary rather than relying on how their work may be described. It has been left to the courts over the years to determine the parameters of the definition. In deciding on the status of a person as employee or self-employed the courts may apply a number of tests.

- The control test—is the person under the control of the employer in carrying out his/her work in terms of how, when and where it is done?
- The integration test—is the person employed as part of the business?
- Is the person in business on his/her own account?
- Is the person exposed to financial risk?

The Code of Practice for Determining Employment or Self-Employment status of Individual is available at *www.revenue.ie/leaflets/revdsw* and provides a useful guide in helping to determine whether a particular person is an employee or not.

In general, a person is an employee if s/he:
- is under the control of another person who decides how, when and where the work is to be carried out;
- provides labour only;
- receives a fixed hourly/weekly/monthly wage or salary;
- cannot sub-contract work to others;
- does not supply materials for the job;
- does not bear a personal financial risk in carrying out the work;
- works set hours or a given number of hours per week or month;
- usually works for one person or one business;
- is entitled to holiday pay/sick pay/pension, etc.;
- receives expense payments to cover subsistence/travel;
- is usually entitled to extra pay or time off for overtime.

In general, according to the Code, a person is self-employed/working under a contract for services if s/he:
- owns the business;
- is exposed to financial risk by having to bear the cost of making good faulty or substandard work carried out under the contract;
- controls what is done, when, where and how it is done;
- is free to hire others on his/her terms to complete the agreed work;
- supplies equipment and materials for the job;
- has a premises where the equipment or materials are stored;
- costs the work and agrees a price;
- provides his/her own insurance cover, e.g. public liability, etc.;
- controls the hours of work in carrying out the job.

An important decision in this area was the Supreme Court case of *Henry Denny & Sons (Ireland) Ltd. v Minister for Social Welfare* [1998] 1 IR 34. The case concerned the status of casual supermarket demonstrators. The demonstrators had written terms and conditions which described them not as employees but as independent contractors responsible for their own tax returns. It was also stated that the Unfair Dismissal Act did not apply to them. Rather than confine itself to the contract, the Court looked at the totality of the situation and decided that the demonstrators were not in business on their own account. Keane J. held as follows:

> It is, accordingly, clear that, while each case must be determined in the light of its particular facts and circumstances, in general a person will be regarded as providing his or her services under a contract of service and not as an independent contractor where he or she is performing those services for another person and not for himself or herself. The degree of control exercised over how the work is to be performed, although a factor to be taken into account, is not decisive. The inference that the person is engaged in business on his or her own account can be more readily drawn where he or she provides the necessary premises or equipment or some other form of investment, where he or she employs others to assist in the business and where the profit which he or she derives from the business is dependent on the efficiency with which it is conducted by him or her.

An interesting case on the amending of terms in a contract was the High Court case of *Finnegan v J & E Davy* [2007] IEHC 18, which concerned the payment of a bonus of €260,296.31. The plaintiff was an accountant who sought to recover a bonus payment arising from his previous employment. He claimed that the defendant sought, unilaterally and retrospectively, to alter the terms of employment in its deferral of a bonus scheme of which he had not been notified. In effect, he would have to work a further two years before becoming eligible to receive a bonus already earned. The defendant argued that the bonus scheme was set up to incentivise staff, to generate loyalty and to try to retain key employees. The court viewed the payment deferral as an attempt to restrict employees who wished to act as stockbrokers from moving to another stockbroking firm. Smyth J. held:

> To enforce a condition it must be fairly and reasonably brought to the other party's attention. This is especially so when in a contract the condition was particularly onerous or unusual (as I find as a fact the deferral and retention of appreciable percentages of bonuses were) and was not known at all to the plaintiff until 1997 and the real and full impact only known to him or impacting upon him until 1998.

The plaintiff had been working for some six years before he was informed of this onerous condition, which in the view of Smyth J. was unreasonable. The learned judge went on to state that the terms of engagement were *'grievously marked by a form of engagement redolent of the indentured employment of another age'*.

The Court found for the plaintiff.

REGULATORY FORA

This chapter will attempt to give an overview of the fora involved in regulating employment law. As the Irish workplace has become more regulated, the fora providing redress for issues have grown, a fact that has not escaped some criticism. The regulatory fora are many and varied; the function and powers of the various bodies range from advisory only to quasi-judicial with decisions binding on the parties.

• Labour Court

Established in 1946 under the Industrial Relations Act 1946, the Labour Court is an independent body consisting of employers' and employees' representatives participating on an equal basis. Since it was first established more than sixty years ago its role has evolved considerably, keeping pace with the significant developments in national and European employment legislation. According to the Labour Court's mission statement, its purpose is to provide fast, fair, informal and inexpensive arrangements for the adjudication and resolution of trade disputes.

When it was first set up the Court did not have the power to make legally binding decisions, except in relation to certain collective agreements. It now enjoys an increased jurisdiction and has the power to make legally binding determinations under a range of Acts.

Structure

The Labour Court has nine full-time members, a Chairperson, two Deputy Chairpersons and six ordinary members (three employer members and three employee members). The Minister for Enterprise, Trade and Employment appoints the Chairperson and the Deputy Chairpersons; the employers' members are nominated by IBEC (Irish Business and Employers' Confederation), while the employees' members are nominated by ICTU (Irish Congress of Trades Unions). The Minister also appoints a legal advisor (Registrar). Hearings generally take place in private before a court of three, comprising a Chair, an employers' member and an employees' member.

Referrals under Industrial Relations constitute the bulk of the Labour Court's work. Ninety per cent of cases were taken under the Industrial Relations Acts, with the remaining 10 per cent referred under a wide range of employment legislation, including part-time and fixed-term contracts. In one case a number of questions have been referred to the European Court of Justice for a preliminary ruling. In 2006 43 per cent of cases concerned complaints by trades unions regarding breaches of Registered Employment Agreements by employers. As such complaints accounted for 1 per cent of cases in 2000, this represents a considerable increase over a five-year period. Disputes where it is not the practice of the employer to engage in collective bargaining were placing particular demands, as can be seen from the *Ryanair* case below. A total of 1,364 referrals was made to the Labour Court in 2006—a drop of 2 per cent from the 2005 figures.

The Labour Court is not a court of law in the strict sense, though it should be noted that it has become more legalistic over the years. In trade disputes the Court acts as a tribunal, hearing both sides and making non-binding recommendations. In cases under legislation relating to the issues listed below the Court has the power to make legally binding decisions:
• employment equality;
• pensions;
• organisation of working time;
• industrial relations (amendment);
• protection of employees (part-time or fixed term);
• national minimum wage.

An important Supreme Court decision on procedures and other issues relating to the Labour Court was that reached in *Ryanair Ltd v Labour Court and IMPACT* [2007] ELR 57.

The background to the case was that Ryanair had tried to enter into various agreements with its pilots concerning retraining and repayment of the costs of that training should they leave the company within five years. The Irish Airline Pilots Association wished to enter into negotiations with Ryanair. The company refused to negotiate directly with unions, stating that it was negotiating with Employee Relation Committees. The pilots refused to negotiate with Ryanair where they could not be represented by their trade union. The matter was referred to the Labour Court. In order to deal with the dispute the Court first had to establish whether or not it had jurisdiction. Were the preconditions in s 2(1) of the Industrial Relations (Amendment) Act 2001 satisfied that:
• a trade dispute existed;
• it was not the practice of the employer to engage in collective bargaining;
• internal dispute resolution procedures had failed to resolve the dispute.

Ryanair argued that the Labour Court lacked jurisdiction in the matter, that there was no dispute and that the referral was part of the applicant's strategy to compel union recognition. It also contended that it had engaged in extensive collective bargaining through its Employee Representative Committees in Townhall Meetings, though it did not negotiate with unions.

The Court found that it did have jurisdiction to hear the case. Ryanair sought to quash that decision by means of judicial review to the High Court on the basis that the preconditions had not been met and that the procedures followed in the Labour Court had been unfair. The High Court refused the order and the matter came before the Supreme Court. In quashing the Labour Court decision, the Supreme Court noted that it had failed to properly investigate the internal dispute resolution mechanism that Ryanair executives claimed it had in place to resolve disputes. A unilateral withdrawal from a process did not mean that there were no collective bargaining arrangements. The Court had erred in its interpretation of what constituted collective bargaining in the company in respect of the group in dispute. The Supreme Court also held that the failure to take sworn or unsworn evidence was a fundamentally unfair procedure. The fact that there had not been disclosure of the identities of the pilots being represented by the union was also deemed unfair.

• Employment Appeals Tribunal (EAT)

The Employment Appeals Tribunal was set up under s 39(18) Redundancy Payments Act 1967. It is a quasi-judicial, tripartite body. Originally set up to adjudicate in disputes relating to redundancy, its scope has been extended considerably over the years. The Tribunal now deals with disputes under the following legislation and statutory instruments:

- Redundancy Payments Acts 1976–2003;
- Unfair Dismissals Acts 1977–2001;
- Minimum Notice and Terms of Employment Acts 1973–2001;
- Maternity Protection Acts 1994–2004;
- Protection of Employees (Employers' Insolvency) Acts 1984–2003;
- Payment of Wages Act 1991;
- Terms of Employment (Information) Acts 1994–2001;
- Adoptive Leave Acts 1995–2005;
- Protection of Young Persons (Employment) Act 1996;
- Organisation of Working Time Act 1997;
- Parental Leave Acts 1998–2006;
- Protection for Persons Reporting Child Abuse Act 1998;
- European Communities (Protection of Employment) Regulations 2000;
- European Communities (Protection of Employees' Rights on Transfer of Undertakings) Regulations 2003;
- Carers' Leave Act 2001;
- Competition Act 2002.

According to the Tribunal's Mission Statement:

> The Employment Appeals Tribunal is an independent body established to provide a speedy, inexpensive and relatively informal means for the adjudication of disputes on employment rights under the body of legislation that comes within the scope of the Tribunal.

The Tribunal comprises a Chairperson and three panels: a panel of Vice-Chairpersons, each member of which is legally qualified and appointed by the Minister; an Employers' Panel, with members nominated by employer organisations; and an Employees' Panel that is nominated by the Irish Congress of Trade Unions (ICTU). The Tribunal ordinarily acts in Divisions consisting of the Chairperson or Vice-Chairperson and two other members, one drawn from each of the other two panels.

Adjudicating on unfair dismissals cases has become the core activity of the Tribunal. According to its 2005 Report, this work accounted for approximately 96 per cent of its workload in terms of time spent at hearings. The Tribunal disposed of 1,381 cases of unfair dismissal in that year. The total number of cases referred to the Tribunal in 2005 was 3,727, an increase of only twenty-seven cases over the previous year. During 2005 Divisions of the Tribunal sat on 229 days, representing 1,141 sittings (527 in Dublin and 614 at various locations outside Dublin). The average waiting period to have a claim heard was twenty-eight weeks in Dublin and forty-one weeks in provincial areas. In order to tackle the backlog, in January 2007 the Minister for Labour Affairs made a number of new appointments and increased the membership of the Tribunal.

The issue of the jurisdiction of the Tribunal arose in the interesting case of *Patricia Mayland v H.S.S Ltd T/A Citywest Golf & Country Club* UD 1438/2004. Following a dismissal, the claimant suffered from panic attacks and was on medication as a result. The claimant asked the Tribunal to take the psychological injuries she had suffered after the dismissal into account. However, the Tribunal determined that the matter was not within its jurisdiction. Note the House of Lords case *Johnson v Unisys Ltd* [2001] IRLR 279, where the Law Lords held that the statutory provision in the UK governing unfair dismissal compensation provides for compensation of *such amount as the Tribunal considers just and equitable in all the circumstances having regard to the loss sustained by the complainant in consequence of the dismissal insofar as that loss is attributable to action taken by the employer*, was not confined to financial loss. It was open to a Tribunal to award compensation, in an appropriate case, for distress, humiliation, damage to reputation in the community or to family life.

• Labour Relations Commission (LRC)

The LRC was established under s 24 of the Industrial Relations Act 1990 and came into being in January 1991 with the purpose of promoting good industrial relations. The function of the LRC is:

> To promote the development and improvement of Irish industrial relations policies, procedures and practices through the provision of appropriate, timely and effective services to employers, trade unions and employees.

To this end the LRC provides the following services:
* an industrial relations conciliation service;
* industrial relations advisory and research services;
* a rights commissioner service;
* a workplace mediation service;
* assistance to Joint Labour Committees and Joint Industrial Councils.

The LRC also has a role to play in reviewing developments in the area of industrial relations, establishing codes of practice and engaging in research.

Conciliation is a voluntary mediation process. It is a very effective means of facilitating the resolution of disputes. When a dispute is referred to the LRC under this process, the LRC assigns an Industrial Relations Officer (IRO) to mediate. The process is informal and non-legalistic. Parties may be represented by trade unions or employer organisations. Settlement of a dispute is by consensus; it is not an outcome that is imposed by the LRC mediator. This service is generally available to all employees and employers, with the exception of the Defence Forces, members of An Garda Síochána and prison officers. Its services are free of charge to employers, employees and their representatives.

* **Advisory Services Division**
The Advisory Services Division is involved in non-dispute situations, where its function is to develop effective industrial relations practices and structures, working in partnership with employers and employees. Services provided include conducting an industrial relations audit in a workplace, providing preventative mediation and preparing codes of practice. Examples of codes of practice cover issues such as grievance and disciplinary procedures, Sunday working in the retail trade and procedures for addressing bullying in the workplace. In 2006 it was involved in 210 projects facilitating the avoidance of disputes in employment.

* **Rights Commissioner**
Rights Commissioners were first established under the Industrial Relations Act 1969. Section 13(2) of the Act set out the functions of the office as being to investigate and to made recommendations in trade disputes. The definition of trade dispute did not include disputes concerned with rates of pay, hours or times of work or annual holidays.

The role of the Rights Commissioner has expanded considerably since the 1969 Act and in recent years has taken on an important and often mandatory role in the resolution of very complex legal issues under seventeen separate pieces of legislation and statutory instruments. The Protection of Employees (Fixed-Term Work) Act 2003 demonstrates such complexity, where the issues are not confined to Irish domestic law but encompass European case law involving, for example, questions of the direct effect of a Directive. Rights Commissioners now investigate disputes and grievances referred by individuals in relation to issues such as leave, employee permits, maternity protection, minimum wage, part-time work, fixed-term work, safety, health and welfare, transfer of undertakings and unfair dismissals. In many instances the Rights Commissioner is the first stop when an individual seeks redress.

Rights Commissioners are appointed by the Minister for Enterprise, Trade and Employment on the recommendation of the Labour Relations Commission. Hearings are generally held in private. They are formal but not adversarial. Parties may be represented, if they wish, by a trade union, an employer's organisation, a solicitor, a friend or a family member. In 2005 the majority of referrals to the Rights Commissioner service (1,875) concerned grievances under the Payment of Wages Act 1991. Referrals in 2006 recorded an increase of 28 per cent over the 2005 figures. These referrals mainly concerned payment of wages, unfair dismissal, hours of work and general industrial relations issues.

The role of the Rights Commissioner under the Protection of Employees (Fixed-Term Work) Act 2003 has been challenged in a number of recent cases. Issues have arisen in cases where complainants sought to rely directly on the Directive of 2001, in respect of events occurring in the period before the passing of the 2003 Act that gave effect to the Directive. Under the doctrine of direct effect a complainant can only rely on a directly effective provision of a Directive before a national court. The question of whether or not a Rights Commissioner can constitute a national court has been referred to the Court of Justice by the Labour Court.

• Workplace Mediation Service

Workplace mediation is a service available to individuals or small groups of workers in situations of conflict, dispute or disagreement in a workplace to enable the parties to arrive at a satisfactory resolution to the difficulties in question. The process is engaged in voluntarily by the parties. The types of situation where mediation could be used include interpersonal differences, issues arising from a disciplinary procedure or certain industrial relations matters.

• Joint Labour Committees/Joint Industrial Councils

The LRC provides Industrial Relations Officers to act as chairpersons to a number of councils and committees. The purpose of the Joint Labour Committees is to draw up proposals in relation to setting minimum rates of pay and conditions for employees in certain sectors. There are sixteen sectors involved, ranging from agricultural workers to catering, contract cleaning, law clerks and tailoring. When the proposals are confirmed by the Labour Court, in the form of an Employment Regulation Order, they become the statutory minimum pay and conditions of employment for the sector concerned. The Joint Labour Committees operate in areas where collective bargaining is not well established.

• Joint Labour Councils

These Councils were established under the 1946 Act. The Act provided that they were associations of employers' and employees' representatives whose function was to bring about harmonious relations between the parties and to facilitate industrial peace. The Act also provided that if a trade dispute arose, the parties would agree not to undertake strike action before such dispute had been referred to the Council for its consideration.

• Personal Injuries Assessment Board (PIAB)

Personal Injuries Assessment Board Acts 2003–2007

The PIAB was set up under the Personal Injuries Assessment Board Act 2003:

> An Act to enable, in certain situations, the making of assessments without the need for legal proceedings to be brought in that behalf, of compensation for personal injuries (or both such injuries and property damage), in those situations to prohibit, in the interests of the common good, the bringing of legal proceedings unless any of the parties concerned decides not to accept the particular assessment or certain other circumstances apply, to provide for the enforcement of such an assessment, for those purposes to establish a body to be known as the Personal Injuries Assessment Board and to define its functions and to provide for related matters.

Section 3 of the Act states that it applies to the following civil actions:

> a)   a civil action by an employee against his or her employer for negligence or breach of duty arising in the course of the employee's employment with that employer
> b)   a civil action by a person against another arising out of that other's ownership, driving or use of a mechanically propelled vehicle
> c)   a civil action by a person against another arising out of that other's use or occupation of land or any structure or building
> d)   a civil action not falling within any of the preceding paragraphs (other than one arising out of the provision of any health service to a person, the carrying out of a medical or surgical procedure in relation to a person or the provision of any medical advice or treatment to a person)

Section 4(1): civil action means personal injuries or both personal injuries and damage to property where both have been caused by the same wrong. In essence, the only personal injuries actions not dealt with by the PIAB are those arising from alleged medical negligence.

Section 11(3)(a): when a person is making a claim for assessment (i.e. an assessment as to the amount of damages the claimant is entitled to) the following must be submitted:

- a document notifying the other side of the claim and seeking compensation;
- copies of any correspondence between the parties;
- medical reports in respect of the personal injury;
- receipts, vouchers or other documentary proof in relation to the loss or damage.

Section 17: the Board has discretion not to arrange for the making of an assessment in a number of circumstances, including the following:

- if in its opinion there is not a sufficient body of case law or settlements to which the assessors could refer for the purpose of making an assessment
- if in its opinion it would not be appropriate to do so because
  - the particular complexity of the issues that would require to be addressed
  - the injuries consist wholly or in part of psychological damage the nature or extent of which would be difficult to determine by the means assessment available to the assessors.

Section 14(2): where a respondent states in writing that s/he does not consent to an assessment being made or, s 32(1)(2)(3), where an assessment has been made and there is non-acceptance by either party in writing, the Board will authorise the claimant to bring proceedings in respect of the claim.

Section 54: one of the functions of the Board is to publish a Book of Quantum containing general guidelines as to amounts that may be awarded in respect of specified types of injury.

Section 56: sets out the membership of the Board, which shall not be more than eleven. They comprise the chairperson and the chief executive, two members nominated by the Irish Congress of Trade Unions, one member nominated by the Irish Business and Employers Confederation, one member nominated by the Irish Insurance Federation, the Director of Consumer Affairs and the Consumer Director of the Irish Financial Services Regulatory Authority.

The 2007 Act came into operation in July of that year. The purpose of the 2007 amending Act was to add two sections to the parent legislation of 2003 in respect of costs, namely ss 51A and 51B.

Section 51A provides that where a claimant rejects an award of damages by the PIAB which has been accepted by the respondent and that award is not exceeded in subsequent proceedings, no award of costs may be made to the claimant. In such proceedings the Court may, at its discretion, order the claimant to pay the defendant's costs. This will not apply if a formal offer (within the meaning of s 17, Civil Liability and Courts Act 2004) is made and the amount is not equal to the PIAB award or if a payment into court of an amount of money or an offer of tender is made.

Section 51B provides that, irrespective of whether an award has been made or accepted, if a claimant brings proceedings in respect of his/her claim, then no amount relating to fees or expenses will be allowed on taxation of costs regarding the PIAB application other than those fees referred to in ss 35, 44 or 45. It has been suggested that this latter provision may be unconstitutional.

• The Equality Tribunal

The Equality Tribunal was set up under the Employment Equality Act 1998. It is an independent body that hears complaints of alleged discrimination under equality legislation. Cases before it come under the Employment Equality Acts 1998–2004, Equal Status Act 2000 and certain sections of the Pensions Acts. The Tribunal is a quasi-judicial body and its decisions are legally binding. In 2006 there was a 12 per cent increase in the number of employment equality cases referred to the Tribunal. These cases concerned discrimination on the grounds of race, age, gender and disability, with the latter two showing a decrease on the previous year's level of referrals.

• Civil Courts

Civil courts also offer a means of redress in employment law issues or in disputes, depending on the nature of the matter in question. The principal courts in this regard are the Circuit Court, the High Court, on rare occasions the Supreme Court and the European Court of Justice.

chapter 3

TERMS OF EMPLOYMENT

> **In this chapter the following areas will be covered:**
> * minimum notice;
> * terms of employment;
> * organisation of working time;
> * payment of wages;
> * minimum wage;
> * part-time workers;
> * fixed-term workers;
> * young persons;
> * protection of employees on the transfer of undertakings;
> * information and consultation;
> * employee permits.

• Minimum Notice and Terms of Employment Act 1973

Section 1 of the Act defines an employee as:

> ... an individual who has entered into or works under a contract with an employer, whether the contract be for manual labour, clerical work or otherwise, whether it be expressed or implied, oral or in writing, and whether it be a contract of service or apprenticeship or otherwise, and cognate expressions shall be construed accordingly.

This Act prescribes minimum periods of notice to be given in the event of termination to an employee who has at least thirteen weeks' continuous service with the same employer.

The Act does not apply to an employee who is a member of the employer's family (father, mother, grandfather, grandmother, stepson/daughter, brother, sister or half-brother/sister), who is a member of the employer's household or whose place of employment is a private dwelling house or farm in which both the employee and employer reside.

The period of notice to which an employee is entitled varies according to length of service, but the Act sets down minimum periods. There is nothing to prevent employers and employees negotiating a greater notice period in a contract of employment. Where such a term exists in a contract, it will apply rather than the statutory period, which is as follows:

> S.4
> (2) (a) if the employee has been in continuous service of his employer for less than two years, one week
> (b) if the employee has been in the continuous service of his employer for two years or more, but less than five years, two weeks
> (c) if the employee has been in the continuous service of his employer for five years or more, but less than ten years, four weeks
> (d) if the employee has been in the continuous service of his employer for ten years or more, but less than fifteen years, six weeks
> (e) if the employee has been in continuous service of his employer for fifteen years or more, eight weeks.

Section 5: provides that an employee has certain rights during the notice period. An employee has the right to be paid during this notice period if available for work, even if there is no work for him/her to do.

Section 7: an employee may waive his/her right to notice under the Act. An employer's right to one week's notice may also be waived.

Section 8: the Act does not affect the right of any employer or employee to terminate a contract of employment without notice because of misconduct by the other party.

Terms of Employment (Information) Act 1994, as amended by the Protection of Employees (Part-Time) Act 2001

This Act amended the Minimum Notice and Terms of Employment Act 1973 and gave effect to Directive 91/533/EEC of 1991 regarding an employer's obligation to inform employees of the conditions applicable to an employment relationship.

The Act applies to all employees who have been in employment with the same employer for more than one month.

Since the enactment of the Protection of Employment (Part-Time) Work Act 2001 the Act also covers part-time workers originally excluded by the 1994 Act.

Section 3 provides that not later than two months after commencing employment the employer:

shall give or cause to be given to the employee a statement in writing containing the following particulars of the terms of the employee's employment

(a) the full names of the employer and employee

(b) the address of the employer in the State or, where appropriate, the address of the principal place of the relevant business of the employer in the State or the registered office as registered with the Companies Registration Office

(c) the place of work or, where there is no fixed or main place of work, a statement specifying that the employee is required or permitted to work at various places

(d) the title of the job or nature of the work for which the employee is employed

(e) the date of commencement of the employee's contract of employment

(f) in the case of a temporary contract of employment, the expected duration thereof or, if the contract of employment is for a fixed term, the date on which the contract expires

(g) the rate or method of calculation of the employee's remuneration

(h) the length of the intervals between the times at which remuneration is paid, whether a week, a month or any other interval

(i) any terms or conditions relating to hours of work (including overtime)

(j) any terms or conditions relating to paid leave (other than paid sick leave)

(k) any terms or conditions relating to –
    (i) incapacity for work due to sickness or injury and paid sick leave, and
    (ii) pensions and pension schemes

(l) the period of notice which the employee is required to give and entitled to receive (whether by or under statute or under the terms of the employee's contract of employment) to determine the employee's contract of employment or … the method for determining such periods of notice

(m) a reference to any collective agreements which directly affect the terms and conditions of the employee's employment

The particulars in (g), (h), (i), (j), (k) and (l) above may be given to the employee in the form of a reference to provisions of statutes or instruments, or of any other laws, or of any administrative provisions or collective agreements. The employee should have a reasonable opportunity of accessing and reading those particulars.

A statement provided by the employer should be signed and dated by, or on behalf of, the employer and a copy retained during the period of the employee's employment and for one year thereafter.

This s 3 repeals ss 9 and 10 of the Minimum Notice and Terms of Employment Act 1973, which related to an employee's entitlement to information about terms of employment.

The statement must indicate the pay reference period for the purposes of the National Minimum Wage Act 2000.

Section 4: provides that where an employee is required to work outside the State for a period of not less than one month, the employer must provide a written statement of particulars, adding the following:

(a) the period of employment outside the State;
(b) the currency in which the employee is to be paid;
(c) any benefits in cash or kind for the employee attendant on the employment outside the state;
(d) the terms and conditions, where appropriate, governing the employee's repatriation.

If any changes are proposed to the particulars, the employer is obliged to inform the employee of the nature and date of any such change not later than one month after the change comes into effect. This does not apply where the changes result from a change in legislation, administrative provisions or collective agreements to which the employer has made reference in the original written statement.

Section 7: covers complaints by employees in relation to breaches of the Act by their employer. It provides that employees may refer complaints to a Rights Commissioner. Appeals may be taken to the EAT, with further appeals on a point of law referable to the High Court.

• The Organisation of Working Time Act 1997

This Act gives effect to Directive 93/104/EC of 1993 concerning certain aspects of the organisation of working time, conditions of employment and the health and safety of workers. The Act sets out statutory rights in respect of maximum periods of working time, rest periods and holidays.

Section 2(1) of the Act defines 'employee' as follows:

> ... a person of any age, who has entered into or works under (or, where the employment has ceased, entered into or worked under) a contract of employment and references, in relation to an

employer, to an employee shall be construed as references to an employee employed by that employer; and for the purposes of this Act, a person holding office under, or in the service of, the State (including a civil servant within the meaning of the Civil Service Regulation Act, 1956) shall be deemed to be an employee employed by the State or Government, as the case may be, and an officer or servant of a local authority for the purposes of the Local Government Act, 1941, or of a harbour authority, health board or vocational education committee shall be deemed to be an employee employed by the authority, board or committee, as the case may be.

Section 3: sets out the categories of employee not covered by the Act, i.e.:
- members of An Garda Síochána or the Defence Forces;
- a person engaged in sea fishing or other work at sea;
- a person who is employed by a relative and is a member of that relative's household, and whose place of employment is a private dwelling house or a farm in or on which he or she and the relative reside;
- a person, the duration of whose working time (saving any minimum period of such time that is stipulated by the employer) is determined by himself or herself, whether or not provision for the making of such determination by that person is made by his or her contract of employment.

Section 11: provides that an employee is entitled to a rest period of not less than eleven consecutive hours in each period of twenty-four hours during which s/he works for the employer.

Section 12: provides for rest periods while at work. An employer may not require a worker to work for a period of more than four hours and thirty minutes without allowing a rest break of at least fifteen minutes. In a period of six hours, a rest break of at least thirty minutes should be provided, which may include the first break. Giving the break at the end of the day does not satisfy this requirement.

Section 13: provides for weekly rest periods, which must be of at least twenty-four consecutive hours. In lieu of this an employer may grant two such rest periods in the next following period of seven days.

Section 14: concerns employees who are required to work on Sundays and the fact of his/her having to work on that day has not otherwise been taken account of in the determination of his/her pay. It provides that compensation must be paid either by a reasonable allowance, by an increase in the rate of pay or by reasonable paid time off or a combination of these.

Section 15: holds that the maximum average working week is not to exceed forty-eight hours. Averaging may be calculated over a four-, six- or twelve-month period, depending on the circumstances in respect of such issues as seasonality of the work or collective agreements—approved by the Labour Court—that may be in place. For most workers the calculating period is four months. This calculating period, referred to as a *reference period*, may not include periods of annual leave or other periods of leave covered under legislation or sick leave.

Section 16: deals with nightly working hours, which are hours between midnight and 7.00am the following day. A night-worker is defined in this section as an employee who:

> (a) normally works at least three hours of his/her daily working time during night-time, and
> (b) the number of hours worked during night-time equals or exceeds 50 per cent of the total number of hours worked by him/her during that year.

The maximum average nightly working hours may not exceed eight hours.

In addition to the provisions of this section, the Safety, Health and Welfare at Work (General Applications) Regulations 2007 require an employer to carry out a risk assessment in relation to work carried out by a night-worker.

Section 17: places an obligation on an employer to provide certain information to an employee in respect of working time. This applies where the contract is silent on the matter. The information that must be provided concerns the specifics of normal starting and finishing times of the employee. If the hours required to be worked include such hours as the employer may from time to time decide—referred to as *additional hours* in the Act—the employer must give at least twenty-four hours' advance notice to the employee. It is interesting to note that it is not necessary for the employer to contact each individual employee because the Act states that posting a notice in a conspicuous position in the place of the employee's employment will be sufficient.

Section 18: is concerned with *zero hours* contracts. Zero hour contracts operate where an employee is either required to be available for work for a certain number of hours or to be available without the guarantee of work. Where an employee does not work the hours, s/he will be entitled to be compensated for 25 per cent of the time s/he is required to be available, or for fifteen hours, whichever is the lesser. The employee must have received advance notice of the requirement to be available for work.

Section 19: provides for annual leave entitlements. The annual leave will be equal to:

- four working weeks in a leave year in which the employee works at least 1,365 hours;
- one-third of a working week for each month in the leave year in which s/he works at least 117 hours; or
- 8 per cent of the hours s/he works in a leave year, subject to a maximum of four working weeks.

Section 20: concerns the time at which leave may be taken within the leave year and provides that it will be determined by the employer, having regard to work requirements and subject to taking into account:

(a) the need for the employee to reconcile work and any family responsibilities;
(b) the opportunity for rest and recreation available to the employee.

Holiday pay is to be paid in advance of the employee taking the annual leave. If an employee is ill on a day of annual leave and produces a medical certificate, that day will not be regarded as a day of annual leave. Where an employee has worked for a period of at least eight months in a leave year, that annual leave should include an unbroken period of two weeks.

The issue of holiday pay arose in *O'Brien's Sandwich Bar v Flanagan* [2006] DWT0614, a case taken on appeal from a decision of the Rights Commissioner.

Facts: the claimant had worked for the respondent for a period of 2.6 hours in February 2005. She attended a trial day, but was deemed unsuitable for the position. As a gesture of good will the company offered her a free lunch. The claimant argued before a Rights Commissioner that she had not received holiday pay and was entitled to an amount equivalent to two years' salary for breach of the Act, amounting to €30,130. The Rights Commissioner found in her favour and awarded her €1.33 holiday pay. This was appealed to the Labour Court, which determined that she should have been paid for the full day in question and that her annual leave entitlement should have been based on a full day's work. This amounted to €4.48, less the €1.33 already paid. Accordingly, the Court awarded her €3.15 under the Act.

Section 21: deals with the entitlement to public holidays. (For details on the nine public holidays available to employees in Ireland, please refer to Chapter 6, Leave.) In respect of a public holiday an employee will be entitled to:
- a paid day off on that day;
- a paid day off within a month of that day;
- an additional day of annual leave;
- an additional day's pay
to be determined by the employer.

In *Thermo King v Kenny* [2006] DWT0611 the issue of sick leave falling on public holidays was examined. The case arose out of an appeal against a decision of the Rights Commissioner.

Facts: the claimant had been employed by the company for ten years and was on certified sick leave from April to September 2003. Under the company's sick leave scheme he was on full pay for the first thirteen weeks of his leave. During this period there were public holidays, for which he was not compensated. The company argued that as the claimant was paid for the days in question through the company's sick-leave scheme, he had the benefit of a paid day off on each public holiday and therefore the company was not in breach of the Act. The Rights Commissioner did not agree:

> S.19 (2) addresses specifically the situation where a day that would be regarded as a day of annual leave, is not regarded as such, if the employee concerned is ill on that day and furnishes to his/her employer a certificate of a registered medical practitioner in respect of his/her illness. No such specific provisions are contained in the Act in regard to public holiday entitlement of an employee who is in receipt of sick pay, in respect of public holidays that fall during his or her sick leave absence.

However, the Rights Commissioner noted the s 21(1) entitlement in respect of public holidays and determined that an additional day of annual leave or an additional day's pay should be provided by the company. The employer company appealed this decision to the Labour Court.

In its determination of the case the Labour Court noted that the payments received by the claimant in respect of the public holidays at issue formed part of his entitlement to sick pay under a collective agreement. The days in question were offset against the total entitlement under the scheme. In those circumstances the Court did not accept that the company could treat those payments as also discharging its statutory obligation to the claimant in respect of the public holidays in question. Accordingly, the Rights Commissioner's decision was affirmed.

Under s 25 there is an obligation on all employers to keep records showing compliance with the provisions of this Act. These records must be kept for a period of at least three years from their making.

The originating Directive allowed for derogations from certain provisions and these were transposed into Irish law through Regulations, including the Organisation of Working Time (General Exemptions) Regulations 1998.

Breaches of the Act may be referred to the Rights Commissioner. Appeals may be taken to the Labour Court with a further right of appeal, on a point of law only, to the High Court.

• Payment of Wages Act 1991
This Act makes a number of provisions in respect of the remuneration of employees.

Section 1 defines an *employee* as:

> … a person who has entered into or works under (or, where the employment has ceased, entered into or worked under) a contract of employment and references, in relation to an employer, to an employee shall be construed as references to an employee employed by that employer; and for the purpose of this definition, a person holding office under, or in the service of the State (including a member of the Garda Siochana or the Defence Forces) or otherwise as a civil servant, within the meaning of the Civil Service Regulation Act, 1956, shall be deemed to be an employee employed by the State or the Government, as the case may be, and an officer or servant of a local authority for the purposes of the Local Government Act, 1941, a harbour authority, a health board or a vocational education committee shall be deemed to be an employee employed by the authority, board or committee, as the case may be.

Section 1 defines *wages* as including any sums payable to an employee in connection with his/her employment, including:

> (a) any fee, bonus or commission, or any holiday, sick or maternity pay, or any other emolument, referable to the employment, whether payable under the contract of employment or otherwise, and
> (b) any sum payable to the employee upon termination by the employer of the contract of employment without his having given to the employee the appropriate prior notice of the termination, being a sum paid in lieu of the giving of such notice.

This definition of *wages* does not include:
- any payment of expenses incurred by the employee in carrying out his/her employment;
- any payment by way of pension, allowance or gratuity in connection with the death, retirement or resignation of the employee or as compensation for loss of office;

- any payment referable to the employee's redundancy;
- any payment to the employee otherwise than in his/her capacity as an employee;
- any payment-in-kind or benefit-in-kind.

Section 2: provides that every employee has the right to a readily negotiable mode of wage payment. The modes of payment prescribed include:
- a cheque, bank draft or other bill of exchange;
- a postal/money order;
- a credit transfer;
- cash.

Section 4: obliges employers to provide each employee with a written statement of wages and deductions with every payment of wages. Where payment is by credit transfer, the statement of wages should be given to the employee as soon as possible after the credit transfer has taken place. The statement must show clearly the gross amount of the wages payable to the employee and must itemise the nature and amount of each deduction. There is an obligation on the employer to ensure that this information is treated in a confidential manner.

Section 5: is concerned with deductions that may be made to wages (or payments received) by an employer, including:
- deductions (or payments) required by law, such as PAYE or PRSI;
- deductions authorised by a term of the employee's contract, such as a pension contribution;
- deductions agreed to in writing in advance by the employee, such as a trade union subscription, credit union or VHI payments.

Deductions may not be made for any act or omission of the employee or for goods and services supplied by the employer the provision of which is necessary to the employment, unless such deduction is covered by a term in the contract, either express or implied, it is fair and reasonable in the circumstances and written details have been given to the employee. Where the deduction is related to the act or omission of an employee, there is the further obligation that the employee must be given at least one week before the making of the deduction, written particulars of the act or omission and the amount of the deduction. Such deductions must be made no later than six months after the act or omission became known to the employer and must be of an amount not exceeding the loss sustained by the employer.
A non-payment of wages is regarded as an unlawful deduction from wages unless the non-payment is attributable to an error of computation.

Complaints under this Act are taken to a Rights Commissioner, with appeals going to the EAT and a further right of appeal, on a point of law only, to the High Court.

• National Minimum Wage Act 2000

This Act came into force on 1 April 2000. Section 2 defines an *employee* as:

> ... a person of any age who has entered into, or works or has worked under, a contract of employment.

The current national minimum hourly rate of pay is €8.65 for an experienced adult worker. This new rate was introduced on 1 July 2007. These statutory minimum hourly rates are gross amounts, i.e. before tax, and PRSI has been deducted.

An experienced adult worker for the purposes of the Act is an employee who is not:

> (i) under 18 years of age; or
> (ii) in the first two years after the date of first employment over age 18; or
> (iii) a trainee undergoing a course that complies with conditions set out in the National Minimum Wage Act 2000 (Prescribed Courses of Study or Training) Regulations 2000.

The Act applies to all employees, full-time, part-time, temporary and casual, with the exception of the following categories:

> (a) the spouse, father, mother, grandmother, grandfather, stepfather, stepmother, son, daughter, stepson, stepdaughter, grandson, grand-daughter, brother, sister, half-brother or half-sister of the employer; or
> (b) apprentices within the meaning of the Industrial Training Act 1967 or the Labour Services Act 1987.

For employees under the age of eighteen years the minimum hourly rate is not less than 70 per cent of the national minimum hourly rate. There are varying rates for employees in courses of study or training and for employees in respect of whom the Labour Court has granted a temporary exemption.

The average hourly rate of pay received by an employee must not be less than the minimum hourly rate of pay to which the employee is entitled. To calculate the average hourly rate, the gross reckonable pay earned by the employee in a pay reference period (be it a week, a fortnight or a month) is divided by the employee's working hours in that pay reference period. A pay reference period may not exceed one calendar month.

Section 8: defines working hours as including overtime, time spent travelling on official business and time spent on training or a course of study during normal working hours and authorised by the employer. Such hours do not include time spent on annual leave, sick leave, protective leave, adoptive leave, parental leave or while laid-off or on strike, or time for which the employee is paid in lieu of notice or time spent travelling between an employee's place of residence and place of work.

Part 1 of the Schedule provides that reckonable pay includes:
- basic salary;
- shift premium;
- piece and incentive rates, commissions and bonuses that are productivity related;
- the monetary value of board and lodgings;
- the amount of any service charge distributed to the employee through the payroll; and
- any payment under s 18 of the Organisation of Working Time Act 1997 on zero hour protection.

Some pay components earned by an employee may not be reckonable in calculating the average hourly rate of pay in order to determine if the minimum hourly rate of pay is being paid.

Non-reckonable pay includes:
- overtime premium;
- call-out premium;
- service pay;
- unsocial hours premium;
- tips and gratuities paid into a central fund managed by the employer and paid through the payroll;
- public holiday premium;
- Saturday premium, Sunday premium;
- allowances for special or additional duties, including those of a post of responsibility;
- expenses, such as travel or subsistence allowances, tool allowance and clothing allowance;
- on-call or standby allowance;
- sick pay;
- holiday pay;
- payment for health and safety leave under the Maternity Protection Act 1994;
- pay in lieu of notice, but not including a payment under zero hour protection;
- any payment by way of a gratuity or an allowance in respect of the retirement or resignation of the employee or as compensation for loss of office;
- pension contributions paid by the employer on behalf of the employee;

- any payment referable to the employee's redundancy;
- any payment-in-kind or benefit-in-kind, except board and lodgings;
- any payment to the employee otherwise than in his/her capacity as an employee;
- compensatory payments for injury or loss of tools or equipment;
- an amount of any award under a staff suggestion scheme;
- loans by the employer to the employee.

Section 22: obliges an employer to keep records demonstrating compliance with the Act in respect of an employee for at least three years from the date of the making of such records.

Section 23: provides that an employee is entitled to a written statement of his/her average hourly rate of pay, reckonable pay, working hours and statutory minimum hourly rate of pay entitlement under the Act in a pay reference period or periods within the previous twelve months, other than the current pay reference period. The employee must put the request in writing and the employer is obliged to respond in writing with the information within four weeks.

Disputes under the Act are referred to the Rights Commissioner. There is a right of appeal to the Labour Court, with a further right of appeal, on a point of law only, to the High Court.

The Georgian Hotel v Fatima Oulidi [2006] MWD063

Facts: the claimant was employed as a housekeeper by the respondent from February 2001 until December 2004. In February 2004 the national minimum wage was increased. The claimant believed she was not receiving the minimum wage and tried to raise the issue with her employer, without success. In 2005 the claimant referred a claim to a Rights Commissioner, who did not uphold the complaint. The claimant brought an appeal against this decision to the Labour Court.

There was a conflict of evidence before the Court. The claimant produced pay slips (not presented to the Rights Commissioner) showing that the hours of work per week amounted to forty. The respondent company produced records showing normal working hours as being thirty-five hours per week. The Court took sworn evidence from the claimant in which she stated that her normal working hours were from 9.00am to 5.00pm five days per week. She took one half-hour break at 3.00pm. The respondent argued that she received one hour unpaid break and worked thirty-five hours per week. It was also argued that the break given to the claimant should not be reckonable as working time and therefore should not be used in calculating her hourly rate. As no witnesses were available for the respondent to give direct evidence as to the hours actually worked and there was no written contract of employment, the Court felt compelled to accept the accuracy of the claimant's testimony in her sworn evidence. The claimant's request for a written statement of reckonable pay, working hours and average hourly rate of pay was not met by the respondent. The Court awarded the Complainant arrears of wages plus expenses.

Section 33: allows the Minister for Enterprise, Trade and Employment to appoint inspectors for the purposes of the Act. Inspectors have powers to enter premises *at all reasonable times,* to make such enquiry as may be necessary, to examine any records and to require persons to answer questions with regard to any matter under the Act. The inspector may not enter a premises without the consent of the occupier unless s/he has obtained a District Court warrant.

Penalties under the Act for breaches include fines and imprisonment for a term not exceeding three years (on indictment), or both.

• Protection of Employees (Part-Time Work) Act 2001

The Protection of Employees (Part-Time Work) Act 2001 came into force on 20 December 2001. Its purpose was to implement Directive 97/81/EC of 1997, concerning the Framework Agreement concluded by UNICE, CEEP and ETUC. In this regard it seeks to ensure that part-time employees are not treated less favourably than a full-time comparator in respect of conditions of employment, unless such unfavourable treatment can be justified on objective grounds. Conditions of employment include, for example, remuneration, pensions, entitlement to sick pay and holiday pay, etc. It provides that all protective legislation applying to full-time employees also applies to part-time employees.

Section 7: defines a part-time employee as an employee whose normal hours of work are less than the normal hours of work of an employee who is a *comparable employee* in relation to him/her. Normal working hours are the average number of hours worked by either a part-time or full-time employee each day during a reference period. A reference period means a period of not less than seven days and not more than twelve months duration.

An employee is a *comparable employee* in relation to the part-time employee if both are employed by the same employer or associated employer. A comparable employee may be of the opposite sex to the part-time employee or of the same sex as him/her. A part-time employee can be compared to a comparable full-time employee where, *per* s 7(3):

> (a) both employees perform the same work under the same or similar conditions or each is interchangeable with the other in relation to the work;
> (b) the work performed by one of the employees is the same or

of a similar nature to that performed by the other and any differences between the work performed or the conditions under which it is performed are insignificant;

(c) the work performed by the part-time employee is equal or greater in value to the work performed by the other employee concerned, having regard to skill, physical or mental requirements, responsibility and working conditions.

In *Bus Éireann v A Group of Workers* PTW/06/7 No.071 2007 the question of same/similar work was examined.

Facts: the case arose by way of an appeal of a Rights Commissioner's decision. A claim was brought on behalf of 189 named part-time school-bus drivers alleging that they were being denied equal pay with full-time bus drivers, contrary to s 9 of the 2001 Act. The Rights Commissioner determined that the claimants did not meet the requirements of s 7(3)(a) and (b) of the Act on the basis that the work of the school-bus driver was not equal in value to that of the regular full-time driver. It was further held that the conditions under which the work of both was performed were significantly different. The complaint was, therefore, not well founded. This decision was appealed to the Labour Court.

The Labour Court found that the work of the part-time driver and the work of the full-time comparator were not carried out under the same or similar conditions:

> While there may be occasions when the part-time school bus drivers drive the regular buses on mainline routes, the Court is satisfied that these occasions are rare and do not fulfill the criteria of interchangeability under the Act.

The Court noted that it was accepted by the parties that the availability of the part-time driver was entirely voluntary, whereas the regular driver was required to:

• work at any location as designated by the company;
• rotate and alternate through roster blocks, which encompass early, late and middle duties;
• undertake rosters which may be changed to reflect variations in customer demands and competitive considerations.

In addition, the Court did not accept that the differences in the work performed by both part-time and full-time drivers was of small importance. The Court went on to examine the work of both groups in terms of s 7(c) and the skill involved, the physical or mental requirements, the level of responsibility and the working conditions.

Skill*:* the Court found that the skill required for full-time regular bus drivers was marginally greater than that required for the part-time school-bus drivers. Both sets of drivers required the same level of qualification to drive, but there were differences in the bus specifications and the conditions under which each worked. The school buses were usually older vehicles, while the standard bus operated by the full-time driver was of a higher specification. The regular bus driver operated on busier city roads, whereas the school-bus driver used non-national, secondary or country roads.

Physical and mental requirements*:* the Court accepted that the physical requirements involved in driving were similar for both grades of driver. Where the mental requirement was concerned, however, the situation was somewhat different. The regular drivers were required to drive different routes, to specific timetables, with a variety of stops on along the routes. As these routes and rosters changed regularly, this placed a significant demand on the driver. An extensive knowledge of routes and timetables was required to deal with passenger enquiries. The school-bus driver did not experience the same level of demand because the school-bus route remained relatively static each year. Unlike the school-bus driver, the regular driver was also required to collect fares, operate a ticketing machine, check passes, reconcile cash and lodge monies with the cash office on a daily basis.

Responsibility*:* the Court accepted that the responsibility for passenger safety was greater for the school-bus driver.

Working conditions*:* these were significantly different. The regular driver was required to be flexible and to change rosters and routes to suit the company's requirements. S/he was required to operate a variety of buses, e.g. city, tour, expressway, on a five-day rota spread over seven days, to change rosters every week, with occasional 5.00am starts. The working hours for the school-bus driver were standard.

Taking all factors into account, the level of responsibility was greater on the regular driver and the working conditions more difficult. The Labour Court therefore upheld the Rights Commissioner's decision that the work of the school-bus driver as a whole was not equal in value to that of the regular driver. Accordingly the Court found that there was no discrimination; the part-time workers were not treated less favourably.

Where the part-time employee is the sole employee, the comparator will be specified in a collective agreement or will be employed in the same industry or sector of employment. If the part-time employee is an agency worker, then the comparable employee is another agency worker.

In *Diageo v Rooney* PTW/03/7 No.042 2004 the central issue was the question of whether or not the claimant was an agency worker or an employee of the company. The case came before the Labour Court by way of an appeal against a Rights Commissioner's decision.

Facts: the claimant was employed as a nurse, working part-time at the occupational health department in the Guinness brewery in Dublin, providing cover for other nurses during sick leave and holidays. She was called in to work when she was required. She alleged that her hours were reduced and she was not paid while on sick leave. The company maintained that she was not an employee but rather an agency nurse and therefore her claim should rest with the recruitment agency. The claimant argued that she had never entered into any contractual arrangement with the IRC (Irish Recruitment Consultants) and that they had merely acted as paying agents of the respondent. She further contended that she worked under the direction and control of the respondent company. In its determination the Court noted:

> A part-time employee can only have a cause of action under the Act if he or she is treated less favourably in respect of their conditions of employment than a comparable full-time employee is treated. If the part-time employee is an agency worker within the meaning of the Act the comparable full-time employee with whom comparison is drawn must also be an agency worker. The term agency worker is defined by S 7 of the Act by reference to the definition of the term contract of employment contained in S 3 . The combined effect of these provisions is that a person who is contracted by the employment agency to supply work or service to a third party, is an agency worker.

The first issue for the Court to determine was whether the respondent, Diageo, or the IRC was the claimant's employer. In examining case law it noted the difficulties highlighted in respect of the employment status of agency workers at common law. Referring to a number of cases, including *Construction Industry Training Board v Labour Force Ltd* [1970] 3 ALL ER 220 and *Minister for Labour v PMPA Insurance* [1986] JISLW 215, it stated:

> These cases highlighted a lacuna in the law. A person on the books of an employment agency could not generally be regarded as an employee of the agency because they did not work under the control of the agency. The client of the agency, for whom the worker did work, could not be regarded as the employer because no contractual relationship existed between them; the only contract being between the agency and the client.
>
> To overcome this anomaly the legal meaning of a contract of employment, and the term employer, was modified in most employment legislation to include contracts, and the parties

> thereto, whereby an individual agrees with an employment
> agency to perform work for a third party.

Upon examination of the facts of the case the Court was satisfied that there was
an offer of employment made by Diageo, which had been accepted by the
claimant. When the claimant became aware of the vacancy for a part-time nurse
with the company, she applied to the sister in charge of the Occupational Health
Centre. She was interviewed and later offered the job. Her hours of work, duties,
responsibilities, rates of pay and other terms had been agreed with the sister. She
was informed that her wages would be paid through the agency, IRC, but she had
never met any person representing the IRC nor did she negotiate with the IRC in
relation to her conditions of employment. The Court was satisfied that the IRC
had been acting on behalf of the respondent company in paying the claimant's
wages from funds provided by the respondent.

The Court went on to apply the control test to the situation: to what extent was
the claimant controlled in her work and who could exercise that control? In this
case the respondent's Director of Medical Services directed the claimant in her
employment at all material times. Pay increases were negotiated with the
respondent. Hours of work and times of work were determined by the
respondent. Accordingly, the Court determined that the respondent company was
the employer and not the agency IRC, therefore full-time nurses employed by the
respondent were comparable employees for the purposes of the Act.

Turning to the substance of the complaint that she was treated less favourably
than a comparator in that she was not paid while on sick leave, the Court upheld
this. On the claim that she was penalised in having her hours reduced the Court
directed that the respondent provide the claimant with access to the same
grievance procedure as was available to comparable full-time employees in order
to process the complaint.

Section 9 of the Act provides that:

> ... a part-time employee shall not in respect of his or her
> conditions of employment, be treated in a less favourable
> manner than a comparable full-time employee.

There is a qualification to this provision. A part-time employee may be treated in
a less favourable manner than a comparable full-time employee if it can be
justified on *objective grounds*.

An objective ground is defined in s 12 as:
> ... based on considerations other than the status of the employee
> concerned as a part-time employee and the less favourable

treatment which it involves for that employee is for the purpose of achieving a legitimate objective of the employer and such treatment is appropriate and necessary for that purpose.

If the treatment of the part-time employee is based on the fact that the employee is part-time, then it is not an objective ground for less favourable treatment.

Less favourable treatment is also allowed in respect of pension schemes. Where an employee works less than 20 per cent of the normal hours of the comparable full-time employee, the right not to be treated in a less favourable manner does not apply in relation to any pension scheme or arrangement. However, this provision does not prevent an employer from entering into an agreement under which part-time employees receive the same pension arrangements as a comparable full-time employee.

In *Mullaney Brothers v 2 Workers* PTW/05/6 066 2006 an appeal of a Rights Commissioner's decision came before the Labour Court. The issue concerned the removal of a half-day Christmas shopping leave from two part-time workers employed by the company.

Facts: the claimants were originally employed in a full-time capacity, but changed to part-time in 2000. As full-time workers they had benefited from the concessionary half-day. According to the company, owing to an error on its part the half-day leave had remained in place when the workers changed their status to part-time, until it was removed in 2004. The company argued that the leave was given on a concession basis to full-time workers who worked six days per week in the two weeks prior to Christmas, to take account of the extra hours' work and to facilitate them in doing Christmas shopping. In November the company informed its staff that the leave would be confined to this category of employee. The benefit was subsequently restored to full-time staff in another sector of the company who worked a five-day week, but not to the claimants.

The Rights Commissioner found in favour of the claimants and directed that they be afforded time off pro-rata to that enjoyed by full-time employees at the company. The company appealed this decision to the Labour Court.

Before the Court the company argued that the different treatment was justified on objective grounds. The contention was that the half-day off was in consideration of the two extra days worked in the run-up to Christmas and was to facilitate staff so affected in doing their Christmas shopping. As the claimants continued their normal attendance during the run-up to Christmas, it was argued that they could not, on that account, claim an entitlement to a facility that applied in consideration of a six-day working week.

The Court did not accept that there was justification on objective grounds. The company failed to satisfy the Court that the half-day was introduced specifically in consideration of a six-day working week. It stated:

> It is clear on the facts of the case that the benefit applied to full-time staff who worked a 5 day week (those in the travel business). Consequently the Respondent's claim that the benefit is solely related to 6 day working is not sustainable. In these circumstances the Court is satisfied that the only basis upon which the benefit was withdrawn from the Claimants is that they were part-time employees. This could not constitute objective grounds within the meaning of section 12 of the Act.

The Court noted that the scope of the benefit was not dependent on hours worked by the employees as it applied equally to employees who worked a five-day week in the travel department and to staff working a six-day week in the drapery department. Consequently, it determined that a pro-rata benefit was inappropriate and instead awarded the claimants a half-day's leave on the same basis as their full-time colleagues.

Section 11: lays down certain provisions in respect of casual employees. A casual employee is a part-time employee who works on a casual basis where:

> (4) (a) (i) he or she has been in continuous service of the employer for a period of less than 13 weeks, and
>
> (ii) that period of service and any previous period of service by him or her with the employer are not of such a nature as could reasonably be regarded as regular or seasonal employment, or
>
> (b) by virtue of his or her fulfilling, at that time, conditions specified in an approved collective agreement that has effect in relation to him or her, he or she is regarded for the purposes of that agreement as working on such a basis.

Employees covered by this section may be treated in a less favourable manner than a full-time comparator in respect of a particular condition of employment if such less favourable treatment can be justified on objective grounds.

Section 13: provides for the review of obstacles to the performance of part-time work. Under this section the Labour Relations Commission is charged with the role of examining every industry and employment sector, at the Minister's request, to identify obstacles facing part-time employment and to make recommendations as to how such obstacles could be eliminated.

Section 15: prohibits the penalisation of employees by the employer for:

- invoking rights in relation to being treated in a less favourable manner than a full-time comparator in respect of conditions of employment;
- opposing, in good faith, unlawful acts under the Act;
- refusing to accede to a request from the employer to transfer from performing full-time work to part-time or vice versa; or
- giving evidence in any proceedings under the Act or notice of intention to so do.

Penalisation is defined as including the dismissal of the employee, unfavourable changes in the conditions of employment or any unfair treatment, including selection for redundancy. In the case of a request to transfer from performing full-time work to performing part-time work or vice versa, action taken against an employee will not constitute penalisation if there are substantial grounds to justify both the employer making the request concerned and the employer taking that action consequent upon the employee's refusal.

Section 16: deals with complaints under the Act. Complaints may be lodged with a Rights Commissioner by an employee (except in the case of a member of the Defence Forces) or, with the employee's consent, by a trade union of which the employee is a member. Written notice of complaint must be presented within six months of the date of the alleged contravention. This time limit may be extended by a further twelve months if the Rights Commissioner is satisfied that the failure to present the complaint within the allotted time was due to reasonable cause. Appeals may be taken to the Labour Court, with a further right of appeal, on a point of law only, to the High Court.

• Protection of Employees (Fixed-Term Work) Act 2003

This Act, which came into operation on 14 July 2003, gives effect to Directive 1999/70/EC of 1999, concerning the Framework Agreement on Fixed-Term Work concluded by ETUC, UNICE and CEEP. The purpose of the Act is to ensure that the principle of non-discrimination applies to fixed-term workers, i.e. that fixed-term workers are not treated less favourably than comparable permanent workers. It also seeks to prevent the abuse of successive fixed-term contracts.

A fixed-term employee is defined under the Act as an employee who has entered into a contract of employment directly with the employer, where the end of the contract concerned is determined by an objective condition, such as arriving at a specific date, completing a specific task or the occurrence of a specific event.

The term *fixed-term employee* does not include employees in initial vocational training relationships or apprenticeship schemes nor employees with a contract of employment that has been concluded within the framework of a publicly supported training, integration or vocational retraining programme. Section 17 provides that the Act does not apply to a member of the Defence Forces, to a trainee Garda or to a nurse. Significantly, unlike the Protection of Employees (Part-Time Work) Act 2001, this Act does not cover employees employed through employment agencies unless such a person is employed under a contract of employment with the agency.

The Act generally applies to any fixed-term employee working under a contract of employment, holding office under or in the service of the State, including a civil servant, employees of a local authority, harbour authority, health board or vocational education committee.

Section 6: provides that a fixed-term employee must not be treated in a less favourable manner than a comparable permanent employee in respect of his/her conditions of employment unless that less favourable treatment can be justified on objective grounds.

Section 7: provides that the objective ground must be based on considerations other than the status of the employee concerned as a fixed-term employee and the less favourable treatment it involves for that employee (which may include the renewal of a fixed-term employee's contract for a further fixed term). It must be for the purpose of achieving a legitimate objective of the employer and such treatment must be appropriate and necessary for that purpose.

Conditions of employment include conditions in respect of remuneration, overtime payments, holiday entitlements and pension rights. Where an employee works less than 20 per cent of the normal hours of a comparable permanent employee, the right not to be treated in a less favourable manner in respect of pensions does not apply.

In *Irish Rail v Stead* FTD052 2005 the Labour Court found that the failure to extend the opportunity to fixed-term employees to join pension and GP medical schemes that were available to permanent employees constituted less favourable treatment. It found that the company had put forward no objective grounds to justify denying fixed-term workers membership of the pension and GP medical schemes. The Court also found that the employee had not been informed of other positions in the department nor been offered opportunities to enhance his career.

In order to ascertain if there is less favourable treatment of a fixed-term employee a comparator must be identified, i.e. a comparable permanent employee.

Section 5: provides that an employee is a comparable permanent employee:

>   (a) if the permanent employee and the fixed-term employee are

employed by the same employer or associated employer and one of the conditions at (i), (ii) or (iii) below is met

(b) where (a) above does not apply (including a situation where the fixed-term employee is the sole employee) the permanent employee is specified in a collective agreement as a comparable permanent employee in respect of the fixed-term employee, or

(c) where neither (a) nor (b) above apply, the employee is employed in the same industry or sector of employment as the fixed-term employee and one of the conditions referred to below is met.

The following are the conditions referred to above:

(i) both the employees concerned perform the same work under the same or similar conditions or each is interchangeable with the other in relation to the work,

(ii) the work performed by one of the employees concerned is of the same or a similar nature to that performed by the other and any differences between the work performed or the conditions under which it is performed by each is so small in relation to the work as a whole or so rarely occur as to be insignificant, and

(iii) the work performed by the fixed-term employee is equal or greater in value to the work performed by the other employee concerned, having regard to such matters as skill, physical or mental requirements, responsibility and working conditions.

Section 8: provides that employers shall inform employees on fixed-term contracts in writing and as soon as is practicable of the objective condition determining the contract, whether it is:

(a) arriving at a particular date;
(b) completing a specific task; or
(c) the occurrence of a specific event.

Section 8(2): provides that where a fixed-term contract is to be renewed, the employee shall be informed in writing of the objective grounds justifying the renewal of the fixed-term contract and the failure to offer a contract of indefinite duration. This information shall be supplied at the latest by the date of renewal.

Section 9: concerns employees on fixed-term contracts who have completed their third year of continuous employment with their employer or associated employer. These fixed-term contracts may be renewed by that employer on only one occasion and any such renewal shall be for a fixed term of no longer than one year.

Where the first contract postdates this Act and the employee has been on two or more continuous fixed-term contracts, the aggregate duration of such contracts shall not exceed four years. Where any term of a fixed-term contract purports to contravene these provisions, that term will have no effect and the contract shall be deemed to be a contract of indefinite duration. However, where there are objective grounds justifying the renewal, this shall not apply.

The term *continuous* was examined recently by the Labour Court in the case of *Department of Foreign Affairs v A Group of Workers* FTD072 2007. This concerned a group of clerical officers employed by the respondent, the Department of Foreign Affairs, and assigned to the Passport Office. Each of the claimants was recruited through public competition, was placed on a panel and engaged as and when temporary positions became available. They were offered fixed-term positions for the period in respect of which their services were required. The claimants had worked under up to thirteen fixed-term contracts. A case was brought before a Rights Commissioner claiming entitlement to a contract of indefinite duration under s 9 of the Act and further claiming that they had been afforded less favourable treatment than a comparable permanent employee in that they had not been paid over the Christmas period. The Rights Commissioner found in their favour. This decision was subsequently appealed by the respondent and came before the Labour Court.

The respondent contended that the condition precedent to the operation of s 9 had not been met by the claimants. As the continuity of the claimants' service had been broken each time the fixed-term contract expired, by a number of weeks or months, none of the claimants had completed his/her third year of continuous service. The claimants argued that the periods between the expiry of one contract and the commencement of another were periods of lay-off and as such did not break the continuity of their employment.

The Court noted that there appeared to be a conflict between s 9 of the Act and Clause 5 of the Framework Agreement from which the Act originated:

> This arises from the fact the Clause 5 of the Framework Agreement applies to fixed-term contracts which are successive thus giving it a considerably wider scope than if its application was confined to employment relationships which were continuous. It seems to the Court that there is a significant qualitative difference between the concept of a continuous employment relationship and one which is successive. The former connotes an employment relationship without interruption whereas the latter indicates a series of relationships which follow each other but can be separated in time.

It went on to note that while the term *successive* is not defined in the Framework Agreement, s 9(5) of the Act states that the First Schedule of the Minimum Notice and Terms of Employment Act 1973 should apply as illustration of what the term means. This provides as follows:

> 1.   The service of an employee in his employment shall be deemed to be continuous unless that service is terminated by
> (a) the dismissal of the employee by his employer or
> (b) the employee voluntarily leaving his employment.
> 2.   A lock-out shall not amount to a dismissal of the employee by his employer.
> 3.   A lay-off shall not amount to the termination by an employer of his employee's service.
> 4.   A strike by an employee shall not amount to that employee's voluntarily leaving his employment.
> 5.   An employee who gives notice of intention to claim redundancy payment in respect of lay-off or short-time shall be deemed to have voluntarily left his employment.
> 6.   The continuity of an employee in his employment shall not be broken by the dismissal of the employee by his employer followed by immediate re-employment of the employee.
> 7.   If a trade or business is transferred from one person to another (whether or not such transfer took place before or after the commencement of this Act) the continuous service of an employee in that trade or business at the time of the transfer shall be reckoned as continuous service with the transferee and the transfer shall not operate to break the continuity of the service of the employee.

The respondent relied on 1(a), arguing that when each of the fixed-term contracts came to an end the claimants had been dismissed, thus the continuity of service had been broken.

The Court noted that while Clause 5(2) of the Framework Agreement allowed Member States to set out the conditions under which fixed-term contracts could be defined as successive, such definition could not render the concept *qualitatively different and narrower in scope than that which the term would normally bear.*

In finding in favour of the claimants, the Court cited *Adeneler and Others v Ellinikos Organismos Galaktos* [2006] IRLR 716 and the finding that a Member State does not enjoy complete discretion, but is bound by the result to be achieved by the Directive and Framework Agreement, which is to prevent abuse of successive contracts. In respect of the respondent's argument the Court stated that it could not apply s 9 of the Act in a way that would defeat the result envisaged by Clause 5 of the Framework Agreement. The Court upheld the Rights Commissioner's decision in holding that the periods between the successive contracts were periods of lay-off and, as such, continuity of service was unbroken. It also held that taking the claimants off the pay-roll over the Christmas period did constitute less favourable treatment.

Section 10: places an obligation on an employer to inform a fixed-term employee when vacancies arise to ensure that s/he has the same opportunity as a comparable permanent employee to secure a permanent position within the organisation. This may be provided by means of a general announcement at a suitable place in the organisation.

In *Scoil Iosagain v Henderson* FTC/04/2 055 2005 a number of issues arose, including the matter of the obligation to inform a fixed-term employee of vacancies arising in a workplace. The case arose by means of appeal from a decision of a Rights Commissioner.

Facts: the claimant was a teacher in a national school. While at a school function in June 2003, he learned that six positions had been advertised in a national newspaper on 29 May. He had not been informed that an advertisement was to be placed or that the vacancies existed and no notice was placed on the staff noticeboard. The day after the function he approached the principal, who indicated that he could not be offered an interview as there were rules and regulations to which the school had to adhere. The claimant subsequently became aware of the provision in the 2003 Act, which came into force the month following his knowledge of the advertisements. His contract of employment with the school ran to the end of August of that year. The matter came before a Rights Commissioner, who determined that as the issue arose before the enactment of the 2003 Act, he did not have jurisdiction to hear the complaint.

This decision was appealed to the Labour Court.

It was argued before the Court that as the State was required to implement the Directive that gave rise to the Act by 10 July 2002, under the Doctrine of Direct Effect the complainant was entitled to rely on the Directive in the proceedings rather than on the Act. On the issue of Direct Effect the Court cited the ECJ case of *Van Gend en Loos v Nederlandse ber Belastingen* [1963] C-26/62, where it was held that the Community constitutes a new legal order that confers rights on individuals that national courts must protect without the need for implementing legislation in the Member States.

In a series of cases, including *Van Duyn v Home Office* [1974] C-41/74, the ECJ further decided that, subject to certain conditions, a Directive could be relied upon independently by an individual before a national court. These conditions were threefold:

1. The relevant provision must be unconditional and sufficiently precise.
2. The time limit for implementing the Directive must have expired without the relevant part of the Directive being correctly and completely implemented into law in the Member State.
3. The action must be against the State.

The respondent did not dispute the presence of the first two conditions, but did dispute the presence of the third. It was argued that the action was not against the State because teachers are employed by the Board of Management of a school rather than by the Department of Education and Science.

On the question of against whom lay the claim, the Court noted that the ECJ had adopted a broad definition of *the State* in case law for the purpose of applying Direct Effect, and had included within that definition bodies that emanate from the State. Examples of such findings included the Chief Constable of a police force in *Johnson v Chief Constable of the RUC* [1986] C-222/84, a local authority in *Fratelli Costanzo v Commune di Milano* [1989] C-103/88 and a state company in *Foster v British Gas plc* [1991] C-188/89.

The Court determined that:

> … it is clear beyond argument that the provision of primary education in a national school is a public service performed under the control of the state. Accordingly the Court is satisfied that the respondent herein is an emanation of the State and that the Directive is directly effective in an action against it.

Citing *Foster v British Gas plc* [1991] C-18/89, the Court considered the opinion of the Advocate General when he stated that:

> … a Member State, but also any other public body charged with a particular duty by the Member State from which it derives its authority, should not be allowed to benefit from the failure of the Member State to implement the relevant provision of a directive in national law.

On the question of informing fixed-term employees regarding vacancies, the Court concluded that the placing of an advertisement in a newspaper did not meet the requirements of either the Directive or the Act:

> What is clearly required is that information on relevant vacancies be imparted personally to fixed-term employees or that a notice be placed in the workplace.

There is a requirement that an employer shall provide access, as far as practicable, to appropriate training opportunities and career development.

Section 13: deals with the prohibition of penalisation of employees who invoke their rights under the Act. These include dismissal, any unfavourable change in the conditions of employment of the employee, any unfair treatment, including selection for redundancy, and any other action prejudicial to his/her employment.

Complaints under the Act are taken to a Rights Commissioner in the first instance, with a right of appeal to the Labour Court and a further right of appeal, on a point of law only, to the High Court.

McArdle v State Laboratory FTC/05/11 No. 63

Facts: the claimant commenced work as a laboratory technician with the respondent in March 2000 on a fixed-term contract for one year. Her job was to assist in the analysis of samples of drivers suspected of being under the influence of drugs while driving. Her contract was renewed on an annual basis thereafter.

The claimant contended that she was provided with terms and conditions less favourable than those applicable to a comparable permanent employee and that she was not provided with a contract of indefinite duration in circumstances where she became entitled to such a contract. She also contended that she was precluded from applying for a permanent vacancy with the respondent. A Rights Commissioner found in favour of the claimant, which decision was appealed by the respondent to the Labour Court.

The Labour Court determined that there were four issues to be decided upon in the case:

1. Could an established civil servant engaged in like work with the claimant be relied upon as an appropriate comparator?

As a temporary civil servant the claimant was classified as an *unestablished* civil servant and as such was not afforded the same entitlements as an established civil servant. The respondent argued that she was entitled to the same conditions as an established civil servant.

The Labour Court found that it is for the claimant to choose his/her comparator, the only proviso being that the criteria under the Act are met. Therefore, the test is whether they are engaged in like work. The fact that one is in a protected category and the other is not is immaterial. It was accepted that at all material times the claimant was engaged in doing the same job as permanent civil servants. Under s 6 a fixed-term employee could not be treated less favourably than a comparable permanent employee.

2. Could tenure be classified as a condition of employment?

The respondent argued that in relation to civil servants, tenure was not a condition of employment as both tenure and conditions of employment were dealt with separately in the Civil Service Regulations Act 1956. The Court noted that the tenure of an established civil servant was up to the age of sixty-five, but their employment could be terminated on certain grounds during that tenure. In the case of the fixed-term employee, tenure was up to the date upon which the contract was due to expire. If the grounds on which it could be terminated during its tenure are a condition of employment, they must be no less favourable than those applicable in the case of a comparator. Citing *O'Cearbhaill v Bord Telecom Eireann* [1994] ELR 54 SC, the Court stated that one would normally expect a contract of employment to contain a term relating to the circumstances in which it could be terminated during its tenure. It was satisfied that such circumstances formed part of the claimant's conditions of employment and, consequently, those circumstances could not be less favourable than those applicable to an established civil servant.

3. What is meant by contract of indefinite duration?

The claimant contended that she ought to have the same tenure as her comparator. The respondent argued that a contract of indefinite duration is a contract that may be terminated on reasonable notice. The Court noted that in accordance with the Act, the term must be given the same meaning as it has in the Framework Agreement:

> It is settled in the law of the Community that a word or expression used in Community legislation must, unless some contrary intention appears, be given a uniform meaning by all Member States, which must take account of the purpose of the provision and linguistic differences *Junk v Kuhnel* ECJ C-188/03 unreported 2005.

The Court found that the expression *contract of indefinite duration* should be understood:

> in contradistinction to a contract of definite duration or a fixed-term contract. The terms and conditions of a contract of indefinite duration which comes into being by operation of S.9(3) must therefore be the same as those contained in the fixed-term contract from which it is derived, as modified by S.6, in all respects other than its fixed duration. Obviously, these terms will vary from one employment to another and every case will be decided mainly on its own facts.

4. Had the respondent contravened the Act by preventing the claimant from applying for a permanent post?

The Court was satisfied that the refusal to allow the claimant to apply for the permanent post flowed directly from the claimant's original status as a fixed-term employee. The Court did not accept the argument that the post was a promotional post rather than a vacancy. Neither did it accept that the complainant's status as an unestablished civil servant was an objective ground on which the treatment complained of could be justified. Relying on her status as an unestablished civil servant was, in reality, a disguised or covert way of relying on the fixed-term status. The claimant had the service and the academic qualifications stipulated for eligibility for the competition. The respondent was in breach of the Act by not allowing the complainant to compete for the vacancy. The decision of the Rights Commissioner was upheld.

The respondent appealed the case to the High Court on a point of law, to the effect that the Labour Court had erred in making or failing to make certain conclusions, the precise nature of which lacked precision. The matter came before the High Court in March 2007, where it was held that the Labour Court had not erred in law. The Court concluded that:

- the employee was entitled to rely on an established civil servant doing like work as a comparator;
- there was an entitlement to the same conditions of employment as an established civil servant, including pension entitlements and access to a career break, but excluding tenure;
- the employee suffered less favourable treatment in being denied the opportunity to participate in the competition for appointment as a chemist.

On the question of the meaning of *contract of indefinite duration*, the Court left the way open to refer a question to the ECJ.

In a 2005 case, *91 Claimants v Various Government Departments*, the Labour Court referred five questions to the ECJ, the results of which will have significant implications in Ireland. Two of the questions go to the jurisdiction of Rights Commissioners/Labour Court, e.g. to hear EU law issues of *direct effect* and whether they constitute *national courts* for the purposes of EU law.

• Protection of Young Persons (Employment) Act 1996, as amended by the Education (Welfare) Act 2000

This Act, which came into force in January 1997, gave effect to Directive 94/33/EC of 1994 on the Protection of Young People at Work and for that purpose repealed the Protection of Young Persons (Employment) Act 1977. The Act also reflects the provisions of international rules drawn up by the International Labour Organisation.

The objective of the Act is to protect the health of young workers by setting minimum age limits for employment, maximum hours of work, rest periods and prohibiting night work for those under eighteen years of age. It also seeks to ensure that work carried out during the school year or during training programmes does not impact adversely on a young person's education.

Under the Act a *child* means a person who has not reached the age of sixteen and a *young person* means a person who has reached the age of sixteen but is under eighteen years of age. The minimum legal working age is sixteen years.

Section 3: permits the Minister for Enterprise, Trade and Employment to authorise, in individual cases, the employment of a child in cultural, artistic, sports or advertising activities not harmful to his/her health, safety or development and which are unlikely to interfere with education or training programmes.

Children over the age of fourteen may be employed to do *light work* during school holidays, provided that:
- the hours worked do not exceed seven hours in any day or thirty-five hours in any week;
- the work is not harmful to the safety, health and development of the child;
- the child does not work for a period of twenty-one days during the summer holidays.

A child over the age of fifteen years may be employed during school term to do light work provided the hours do not exceed eight hours in any week. Persons over fifteen years may be employed as part of an approved training programme. Work experience is also allowed under the Act, provided the hours do not exceed eight hours in a day or forty hours in a week.

Section 4: provides that an employer shall not employ any child on any work between 8.00pm on any one day and 8.00am on the following day.

Rest periods for a child are prescribed as follows:
- a minimum rest period of fourteen consecutive hours in each period of twenty-four hours;
- a minimum rest period of two days in any period of seven days, as far as practicable to be consecutive;
- a break of thirty consecutive minutes after four hours' work.

Section 5: obliges an employer to require production of proof of age before employing a young person or child. In the case of a child the written permission of the parent or guardian must be obtained. The employer must maintain a register in relation to each child or young person employed, detailing the date of birth, time s/he commences and finishes work each day and rates of pay.

Section 6: prohibits an employer from, in general, requiring a young person to work for more than eight hours in any one day or forty hours in any one week. There is also a prohibition on working between 10.00pm on any day and 6.00am the following day. Where the work is during school holidays or on weekend nights when there is no school the following day, a young person may work up to 11.00pm.

Rest periods are prescribed as follows:
- a minimum rest period of twelve consecutive hours in each period of twenty-four hours;
- a minimum rest period of two days in any period of seven days, as far as practicable to be consecutive;
- a break of thirty consecutive minutes after four-and-a-half hours' work.

These rest periods do not apply in the shipping or fishing sectors.

Section 9: allows for the modification of certain provisions of the Act where the child or young person is employed by close relatives in a family business or farm, provided the health, welfare and safety of the employee is not endangered.

Section 10: where a person under eighteen years of age works for more than one employer, the combined daily or weekly hours of work do not exceed the maximum set out above.

Section 12: requires an employer to display the prescribed abstract of the Act at the principal entrances to work premises.

Under the Health, Safety and Welfare at Work Regulations 2007 an employer is obliged to carry out a risk assessment.

Complaints under the Act are dealt with initially by a Rights Commissioner, with a right of appeal to the EAT and a further right of appeal, on a point of law only, to the High Court.

Inspectors with wide-ranging powers may be appointed by the Minister. These inspectors may enter any premises, make any enquiry or examination, require records to be produced and require an employee and employer to answer any questions (other than questions tending to incriminate) as the inspector may put to them.

• The European Communities (Protection of Employees on Transfer of Undertakings) Regulations 2003

The purpose of these Regulations is to protect the contractual rights of employees in respect of their employment in the event of a transfer to another employer of the business, or part of the business in which they are employed, as a result of a legal transfer or merger. The Regulations gave effect to Directive EC/2001/23 and revoked the earlier Regulations. They apply to all entities, public or private, engaged in economic activities, whether for profit or not. They do not apply to sea-going vessels.

Section 2: defines *transfer* as '*the transfer of an economic entity which retains its identity*'.

An *economic entity* is further defined as meaning '*an organized grouping of resources which has the objective of pursuing an economic activity whether or not that activity is for profit or whether it is central or ancillary to another economic or administrative entity*'.

In *Dr Sophie Redmond Stichting v Bartol* 1992 C-29/91 the plaintiff was a Foundation engaged in the provision of assistance to drug addicts in Holland, and the defendants were its employees. The local authority in the Municipality of Groningen, which granted the Foundation subsidies (its sole resources), ceased to do so with effect from 1 January 1991. The subsidies were transferred to another Foundation engaged in assisting drug addicts, namely the Sigma Foundation.

The Redmond Foundation, which was now without any resources, applied to the Kantongerecht, Groningen, under Art 1639w of the Civil Code to set aside its contracts of employment with such members of its staff as were not taken on by the Sigma Foundation. The issue was the question of whether or not a transfer had taken place.

The ECJ set out a checklist for consideration when determining whether the entity in question had retained its identity. These include:
- the type of undertaking concerned;
- whether its tangible or intangible assets are transferred;
- whether its employees and/or customers are transferred;
- the level of similarity between the activities carried on.

Under these Regulations the rights and obligations of the original employer (the transferor) arising from a contract of employment existing at the time of the transfer shall be transferred to the new employer (the transferee). Following a transfer, the transferee is obliged to continue to observe the terms and conditions agreed in any collective agreement until the date of expiry of the agreement or the entry into force of a new collective agreement. These terms and conditions do not include rights to old age, invalidity or survivors' benefits under supplementary company nor to inter-company pension schemes outside the Social Welfare Acts. Pension rights not transferred across to the new contract are protected under the Pension Acts 1990–2003, where they are approved pension schemes and so come within the meaning of those Acts. Unapproved occupational pension schemes are required to be protected by the transferee.

Section 6: where the transferor is subject to bankruptcy or insolvency proceedings the rights and obligations do not apply. However, if the sole or main reason for the bankruptcy or insolvency proceedings is the evasion of an employer's legal obligations under the Regulations, then the Regulations will apply to the transfer.

Section 5: prohibits dismissal by reason of the transfer of a business. This does not include dismissals for '*economic, technical or organizational reasons which entail changes in the workforce*'. Employees dismissed contrary to this provision may have redress under the Regulations or under the Unfair Dismissals Acts, but not under both.

If the transfer involves a substantial change in the working conditions of an employee to the detriment of the employee concerned, then the employer will be regarded as having been responsible for the termination of the contract of employment. Such circumstances could give rise to a claim for constructive dismissal under the Unfair Dismissals Acts or under the Regulations.

Section 8: provides for information and consultation in the event of a transfer. The transferor and the transferee are both obliged to inform their respective employees' representatives of the following:
- the date of the transfer;
- the reasons for the transfer;
- the legal, economic and social implications of the transfer for the employees;
- any measures envisaged in relation to the employees.

This information must be supplied not later than thirty days before the transfer is carried out. Where there are no representatives, a process must be put in place whereby the employees may choose representatives. If there are still no representatives, each of the employees must be informed in writing, where reasonably practicable, of the facts above.

Breaches of the Regulations may be taken to a Rights Commissioner within six months, with a right of appeal to the EAT.

• Employees (Provision of Information and Consultation) Act 2006

This Act gives effect to Directive 2002/14/EC by providing for the establishment of arrangements for informing and consulting employees in undertakings or businesses that have at least fifty employees. It also gives effect to Directive 2001/23/EC on the safeguarding of employees' rights in the event of the transfer of undertakings or businesses.

Section 4: sets out details of the application of the Act on a phased basis:
- undertakings with at least 150 employees from 4 September 2006 by virtue of S.I. 383 of 2006;
- undertakings with at least 100 employees from 23 March 2007;
- undertakings with at least 50 employees from 23 March 2008.

Section 5: sets out how the number of employees, or *relevant workload threshold,* is to be calculated. The calculation is based on the average number of employees employed in an undertaking during a two-year period. If the undertaking has been in existence for less than two years, the calculating period is the period for which the undertaking has been in existence.

Section 7: concerns the process for establishing information and consultation arrangements and states that the employer:

(a) may at his or her own initiative, or
(b) shall, at the written request of at least 10 per cent of employees received either by him or her on the one hand, or by the Court or a nominee of the Court on the other hand,
enter into negotiations with employees or their representatives (or both) to establish information and consultation arrangements.

The Act provides for three types of information and consultation agreement:
- negotiated agreements;
- pre-existing agreements;
- Standard Rules.

Negotiated Agreements

Section 8 enables the employer and employees, or their representatives, to devise their own information and consultation agreement through negotiation. A negotiated agreement is in writing, dated, signed by the employer, approved by the employees and applicable to all employees to whom the agreement relates. Approval by the employees means approval by a majority of the employees or their representatives. Negotiated agreements must include the following details: the duration of the agreement and procedures for renegotiation; the subjects for information and consultation; the method and timeframe by which information is to be provided and consultation is to be conducted; and the procedure for dealing with confidential information. At any time before the agreement expires, or within six months of its expiry, the parties to it may renew it for any further period they deem suitable.

Pre-Existing Agreements
Section 9: refers to pre-existing agreements, which may be retained provided certain conditions are met. A pre-existing agreement is one that was in place:
- in undertakings with at least 150 employees on or before 4 September 2006;
- in undertakings with at least 100 employees on or before 23 March 2007;
- in undertakngs with at least 50 employees on or before 23 March 2008.

Like the negotiated agreement, the pre-existing agreement must be in writing, dated, signed by the employer, approved by the employees and applicable to all employees to whom the agreement relates. Details which must be present include references to the duration of the agreement and procedures for renewal, the subjects for information and consultation and the method by which information is to be provided and consultation conducted. Where a pre-existing agreement has expired for six months or more, employees may make a request for negotiations.

Standard Rules
Section 10: sets out when the Standard Rules apply. They will apply in the following circumstances:
- where the parties agree to adopt them;
- where the employer refuses to enter into negotiations within three months of receiving a written request from employees or notification of a valid request from the Labour Court, as provided for under s 7; or
- where the parties cannot agree to the establishment of an information and consultation arrangement within the time period specified in s 7 of six months, which may be extended by the parties' agreement.

The Standard Rules are set out in Schedule 1 and 2 of the Act.

Section 11: provides that, in relation to negotiated agreements and pre-existing agreements, employees may exercise their rights to information and consultation either directly or through their representatives elected or appointed for that purpose. There are certain conditions that must be met if there is to be a changeover from direct involvement to representation.

Section 12: requires that when arrangements are being made for information and consultation under the Act, the employer and one or more employees or representatives shall work in a spirit of co-operation, having due regard to their reciprocal rights and the interests of both the undertaking and the employees.

Section 13: concerns the protection of employees' representatives. It prohibits an employer from penalising employees' representatives for carrying out their functions under the Act. Penalisation is defined as dismissal, any unfavourable change in conditions of employment, any unfair treatment, including selection for redundancy, and any other action prejudicial to his or her employment. Reasonable facilities, including time off, shall be given to employees' representatives to enable them to carry out their duties. The granting of such facilities shall have due regard to the size and needs of the undertaking concerned.

Section 14: provides that parties to the information and consultation process, including experts providing assistance, are prohibited from disclosing confidential information to employees or third parties, unless those parties are subject to a duty of confidentiality.

An employer may refuse to communicate information or undertake consultation where the nature of that information or consultation is such that it would seriously harm the functioning of the undertaking or be prejudicial to the undertaking.

Section 15: disputes under the Act are treated in a number of ways depending on the nature of the dispute.

Disputes concerning:
- negotiated agreements or an agreement under the Standard Rules;
- the interpretation or operation of a pre-existing agreement or a negotiated agreement;
- the interpretation or operation of the Standard Rules or the procedures for the election of employees' representatives; and
- the interpretation or operation of a system of direct involvement

are referred to the Labour Court only *after* going through an internal dispute resolution procedure (if any), a reference to the Labour Relations Commission and a certificate from that body stating that resolution is not likely at that forum.

Disputes arising out of an employer's refusal to communicate information or undertake consultation or breaches of the confidentiality rule under s 14 may be referred to the Labour Court by the employer, by one or more employees and/or by their representatives. Appeals may be referred to the High Court on a point of law only.

• Employment Permits Act 2003–2006

This Act provides for the granting of employment permits to certain foreign nationals to enable them to work in the State. A foreign national means a person who is not a citizen of the State.

Section 2: states that a foreign national shall not enter the service of an employer in the State or be in employment in the State except in accordance with an employment permit granted under the Act. This requirement applies whether the employment results from the foreign national being employed in the State or being employed by a person outside the State but performing duties in the State, the subject of an agreement between a contractor and another person.

Section 2 *does not apply* to the following:
- a non-national who has been declared to be a refugee under s 17 of the Refugee Act 1996;
- a non-national who is entitled to be in the State under s 18 or s 24 of the Refugee Act 1996. Such persons include members of the refugee's family. Where the refugee is under eighteen years of age and unmarried, it includes his/her parents;
- a non-national who is entitled to be in the State under s 24 of the Refugee Act 1996. Such persons include *programme refugees*, i.e. non-nationals who are in the State for the purposes of temporary protection;
- a non-national who is entitled to enter the State and to be in employment in the State pursuant to the Treaties governing the European Communities;
- a non-national who is permitted to remain in the State by the Minister of Justice, Equality and Law Reform and who is employed in the State pursuant to a condition of that permission.

Notwithstanding the above, there are restrictions, for the time being, on non-nationals who are nationals of Bulgaria and Romania. In line with other EU Member States, Ireland has decided to temporarily restrict free access to the Irish labour market for such individuals, at least until the end of 2008. The Minister may lift such restrictions by order if it is in the interests of the proper functioning of the economy to make such an order. Preference will be given to nationals from Bulgaria and Romania over non-EEA nationals in respect of applications for work permits.

Applications for the grant of an employment permit may be made by the person proposing to employ the foreign national, or by the non-national where there is an offer of employment in writing within such period preceding the application as may be prescribed. In certain circumstances applications may be made by a contractor (a person outside the State) or by a party to an arrangement relating to the foreign national.

Section 6: concerns applications made other than by a non-national and stipulates that the following information must be provided:
- a full description of the employment and the terms and conditions, including hours per week, place of the employment and the duration of the employment;

- remuneration and any deductions, where agreed, for board and accommodation;
- qualifications and skill required;
- documentation showing qualifications, skills or experience of the foreign national concerned;
- detail whether or not the foreign national has sought permission to enter the State previously or has been in the State previously without permission;
- where the foreign national is in the State, documentation relating to the permission granted to be in the State.

Section 7: where the application is made by the foreign national the following shall be provided:
- documentation showing skills, qualifications and experience as may be requested by the Minister for Enterprise, Trade and Employment;
- details of past applications to enter the State and whether or not s/he has been in the State on a previous occasion without permission;
- documentation relating to a permission to enter the State where the foreign national is in the State at the time of application;
- details of the offer of employment and the skills, qualifications and experience required;
- details of the place of employment;
- details of the proposed remuneration and any deductions, where agreed, for board and accommodation;
- any other information prescribed by the Minister to support the application.

In 2007 (up to September) the top eight countries' nationals in receipt of permits were:

India	2,559	(1,764 new permits, 795 renewals);
Philippines	2,474	(774 new permits, 1,700 renewals);
South Africa	981	(398 new permits, 583 renewals);
Ukraine	955	(249 new permits, 706 renewals);
USA	822	(587 new permits, 235 renewals);
China	763	(211 new permits, 552 renewals);
Brazil	708	(162 new permits, 546 renewals);
Australia	581	(306 new permits, 275 renewals).

Section 8(5): generally the period specified in the permit shall not exceed two years.

Section 20(3): renewals of permits are generally for a period not exceeding three years. If, however, at the time of application the permit (including a renewal period) has been in force for five years or more, the period for which the permit may be renewed on foot of that application may be an unlimited period.

Section 23: prohibits an employer from making deductions from the remuneration of a permit-holder for expenses arising out of the application or renewal of the permit, out of recruitment of the holder or for any amounts previously paid to the holder in respect of travelling expenses to take up the employment.

Section 23(3): prohibits the retention by an employer or person who made the offer of employment of personal documentation belonging to the holder. Personal documentation includes a passport, travel documents, driving licence, identity card, a document relating to any account with a financial institution or a document relating to the skills, qualifications or experience of the employer.

chapter 4

SAFETY, HEALTH AND WELFARE
IN THE WORKPLACE

> This chapter will examine the historical background to health and
> safety law in Ireland. It will consider the sources of such law, case law
> and legislation, with particular emphasis on the Safety, Health and
> Welfare at Work Act 2005.

According to a report by Indecon International Economic Consultants,
occupational injury and illness costs the Irish economy up to €3.6 billion per
year or 2.5 per cent of GNP. The report, commissioned in 2006 for the
Department of Enterprise, Trade and Employment, undertook an economic
assessment of the effect of occupational safety, health and welfare law on the Irish
economy since 1989, and particularly on competitiveness. In its *Summary of
Injury, Illness and Fatality Statistics Report 2005–2006,* the Health and Safety
Authority concluded, from statistics produced in 2004, 2005 and 2006, that
recurring risks appear in particular areas:

* the construction sector consistently has the highest rate of injuries causing
  more than three days' absence from work;
* the hotel and restaurant sector suffers a high proportion of injuries to non-
  Irish national workers;
* the health, social work and public administration sectors suffer a high
  proportion of violent incidents;
* manual handling triggers one-third of all reported incidents;
* over 20 per cent of all reported incidents result in back injuries;
* elderly agricultural workers suffer a high fatality rate.

The Central Statistics Office (CSO) estimates that over 1.6 million work days
were lost in 2005 due to occupational injury and illness. Most reported incidents
(30 per cent) involve *labourers, mining, construction, manufacturing* and *transport.*
The number of injuries reported for non-Irish workers increased from 700 in
2005 to over 800 in 2006, representing over 10 per cent of all reported injuries.
In 2006, 34 per cent of all reported injuries were triggered by manual handling;
slip, trip and fall incidents were the second most common type of injury in 2006,
similar to 2004 and 2005. Public administration, defence, health and social-work
sectors reported particularly high levels of violent incidents (*Summary IIFS
report*).

In addition to the economic loss, there is the real human cost sadly experienced by those individuals and their families who suffer workplace injuries and illnesses each year, some fatal. The *Annual Health and Safety Authority Report 2006* recorded fifty deaths resulting from accidents in the workplace, a decrease from the 2005 figure of seventy-four. Of these, forty-four were worker fatalities, representing a decrease of 35 per cent on the fatality rate recorded in 2005. Most of these fatal accidents resulted from victims being trapped or crushed by an object or machinery; from injuries sustained from falling, moving or flying objects; from falls from heights; and from injuries caused by vehicles in the workplace. Agriculture and construction continue to be the high-risk industries in this regard. The number of construction-related deaths fell by almost 50 per cent, with twelve in 2006—down from twenty-three in 2005. The farming sector suffered eighteen deaths in 2006 (sixteen of which were workers)—the same number as in 2005. It is estimated that there are approximately 34,000 persons not in the labour force due to occupational injury or illness.

Non-Irish workers continued to suffer a higher rate of fatal accidents in 2006 compared to Irish workers. Of the total of fatal-injury victims, 84 per cent were Irish, 14 per cent were from other EU States and 2 per cent were from non-EU countries. The Central Statistics Office (CSO) estimates that non-Irish nationals constitute 10 per cent of the Irish labour force.

In 2005 these fatalities occurred mainly in construction, while in 2006 they occurred across a range of economic sectors: manufacturing (2), transport (2), fishing (1), construction (1), other personal services (1), wholesale and retail trade (1). Eleven of the fifty fatalities occurred in Cork, six in Clare and four each in Donegal and Dublin. Over 25 per cent of fatality victims in 2006 were aged over sixty-five years and most of these were in agriculture.

The most recent data from Eurostat on the EU 15 and the EU Area suggests that Ireland's health and safety performance is positive in the European context, with the fatality rate ranking below the average for the EU 15. The rate of non-fatal incidents is *consistently one of the lowest in Europe,* with 1,126 incidents per 100,000 in 2004, where the EU 15 average was 3,211 incidents per 100,000. Only The Netherlands had a lower rate. France and Luxembourg had the highest at over 4,000 per 100,000 (*HSA Summary Report,* pp. 53–4).

• Sources of Safety Law
The law on health, safety and welfare at work is to be found in a number of sources: the Safety, Health and Welfare at Work Act 2005, the Safety, Health and Welfare at Work (General Application) Regulations 2007 and a considerable body of case law. Workplace safety and health has been a significant element of EU social policy over the years, with a number of EC Directives giving effect to those policy initiatives—most notably the 1989 Framework Directive. There is

now a considerable range of Directives in place covering particular sectors or risk groups.

Issues of safety, health and welfare in the workplace had been covered by common law for many years, but it was not until 1989 that a legal framework was set down establishing, for the first time, minimum standards for all workplaces. Before 1989 minimum standards had been established for specific areas of work, most notably the Factories Act 1955, the Safety in Industry Act 1980, the Mines and Quarries Act 1965 and the Office Premises Act 1958, in addition to a plethora of regulations. As a consequence, the approach was quite fragmented. A further limitation was the fact that approximately only 20 per cent of the workforce was covered by the legislation; agriculture, forestry, fishing, transport, laboratories and hospitals were excluded from the provisions of such legislation. Calls for reform led to the establishing of the Barrington Commission in 1983, comprising employers, trade unions, government representatives and other interests under the chairmanship of Mr Justice Donal Barrington. The report that issued from that group ultimately led to the passing of the Safety, Health and Welfare at Work Act in 1989. This mirrored a similar process in the UK where, as a result of the Robens Committee reporting in 1972, the 1974 Health and Safety at Work Act was passed.

One major recommendation of the Barrington Report was that a system be put in place that would be preventative rather than reactive. The Report stated:

> It is not merely that prevention is better than cure. Once an accident has happened there is often no cure. If a system is to be preventative, safety must be a feature in the planning of factories and systems of work.

• Common Law

Under common law, duties were placed on employers going back some 100 years, but common law provided a remedy only in the event of a workplace accident; it was curative rather than preventative. The employer was not expected to guarantee the safety of his/her employees. It was not an unlimited duty: the employer was required to ensure the safety of his/her employees only insofar as it was reasonably practicable to do so.

Common law duties imposed on an employer were:
- the duty to provide competent staff;
- the duty to provide a safe place of work;
- the duty to provide and maintain proper equipment;
- the duty to provide a safe system of work.

The Courts interpreted the term *reasonably practicable* to mean:

> The law does not require an employer to ensure in all circumstances the safety of his workmen. He will have discharged his duty of care if he does what a reasonable and prudent employer would have done in the circumstances.
> (Henchy J. in *Bradley v CIÉ* [1976])

One of the best statements of this general principle is to be found in *Stokes v Guest, Kean and Nettlefold (Bolts & Nuts)* [1968] 1 WLR 1776, where Swanwick J. stated:

> ... the overall test is still the conduct of the reasonable and prudent employer, taking positive thought for the safety of his workers in the light of what he knows or ought to know; where there is a recognised and general practice which has been followed for a substantial period in similar circumstances without mishap, he is entitled to follow it, unless in the light of common sense or newer knowledge it is clearly bad; but where there is developing knowledge, he must keep reasonably abreast of it and not be too slow to apply it; and where he has in fact greater than average knowledge of the risks, he may be thereby obliged to take some more than the average or standard precautions. He must weigh up the risk in terms of the likelihood of injury occurring and the potential consequence if it does; he must balance against this probable effectiveness of the precautions that can be taken to meet it and the expense and inconvenience they involve. If he is found to have fallen below the standard to be properly expected of a reasonable and prudent employer in these respects, he is negligent.
> (p. 72 *ELR*, Vol. 16, No. 2, 2005)

In this case the plaintiff, Stokes, contracted cancer of the scrotum from exposure to mineral oil at work over a long period of time. The oil saturated his clothing and came into contact with his skin on a daily basis. The factory doctor was aware of the cancer risk, but no steps were put in place to address it. Stokes eventually died from the cancer.

The duty did not limit itself to the physical well-being of the employee. In recent years the focus has begun to shift to other forms of work-related injury, including stress and recognised psychiatric injury.

In *Curran v Cadbury (Ireland) Ltd* [2000] 2 ILRM 343, McMahon J. stated:

> The duty of the employer towards his employee is not confined to protecting the employee from physical injury only; it also

extends to protecting the employee from non-physical injury such as psychiatric illness or the mental illness that might result from negligence or from harassment or bullying in the workplace. In *Walker v Northumberland County Council* ... the English courts imposed liability where the plaintiff foreseeably suffered a nervous breakdown because of unreasonably stressful working conditions imposed on him by his employer. There is no reason to suspect that our courts would not allow this line of authority if it came before the courts in this jurisdiction.
(p. 78, *ELR*, Vol. 16, No. 2, 2005)

The case is important because it was the first occasion in recent years when the Courts had the opportunity to consider the issue of nervous shock.

Facts: the plaintiff, who had been employed by the defendant for sixteen years, was working with another employee near a conveyor belt that carried chocolate bars to her work-station, where they were packed by the plaintiff and her fellow worker. On the date in question the conveyor belt was switched off, but the plaintiff was not informed of this. She had been away from her work-station at the time. On her return she switched it back on and, hearing screams and commotion, suddenly realised there was a fitter inside the machine carrying out repairs. She thought she had killed the fitter. She claimed to have suffered a serious psychiatric illness as a consequence.

McMahon J. stated that:

> ... [she] was a participant in, and not a mere observer of, the accident. She started the machine. She pressed the button. She heard the commotion and the screams, since the fitter, although out of sight, was quite close to her. She unwittingly caused the injuries to the fitter. Thinking she had killed or seriously injured her fellow employee she quickly turned off the power and then ran some 45 yards around the machine to see the result of her work. As she ran, she was filled with fear, apprehension and, probably, irrational guilt. Her evidence was that when she arrived at the scene where the fitter was she was blinded with panic. She could not see the fitter's face. All she saw was a blur where his face was and she became aware of a person frantically trying to get out of his overalls: she had cause to fear the worst.

It was held that the facts clearly showed that she was a primary victim as opposed to a secondary victim. She was at the very centre of the frightening episode. She was not a secondary victim, i.e. a person who was not involved in the accident itself but who was removed from the direct action or came upon the immediate aftermath of the accident.

Referring to the definition of *personal injury* in the Safety, Health and Welfare at Work Act, the judge noted that no distinction was made between physical and psychiatric injuries. The medical evidence of two doctors was that the plaintiff had suffered from mild to moderate post-traumatic stress disorder, a recognisable psychiatric illness in this jurisdiction. The employer was held to be in breach of its common law duty of care to the employee as well as its statutory duty under the Safety, Health and Welfare at Work (General Application) Regulations 1993. It was held that the plaintiff was entitled to recover on that ground because it was reasonably foreseeable to the defendant that an employee might suffer psychiatric injury as a consequence of that breach of statutory duty.

As stated earlier, the common law duties imposed on an employer comprise the following:
- the duty to provide competent staff;
- the duty to provide a safe place of work;
- the duty to provide and maintain proper equipment;
- the duty to provide a safe system of work.

Competent Staff
The employer's duty in this regard is mainly concerned with the selection of the workforce. An employer should give careful consideration to the qualifications and experience of prospective employees at the recruitment stage to ensure that competent staff members are engaged. The employer's duty also extends to monitoring performance, supervision and disciplinary procedures.

Safe Place of Work
An employer has a duty to ensure that employees have a reasonably safe place in which to work. *Fletcher v Commissioners of Public Works* [2003] SC is an example of a case concerned with the failure to provide a safe place of work.

Facts: the plaintiff was first employed by the defendants in 1977 and was engaged in Leinster House as a general operative from 1985, helping plumbers, electricians and fitters in the maintenance of what described as '*an enormous and labyrinthine central heating system*'. It was accepted by the court that the piping in the system was '*covered with a lagging containing asbestos of various types and that much of it was in an extremely poor condition i.e., it was friable, dusty and falling off in many places*'.

As part of his work he was required to hack off the lagging to facilitate access to the piping for the maintenance people he was assisting. This was done in difficult conditions, in very confined spaces. It was accepted as fact that significant quantities of asbestos polluted the air and that large quantities of asbestos dust were inhaled by the plaintiff over a number of years. This situation continued until 1989.

In July 1984 an inspection was carried out on behalf of the Minister for Labour and the conclusion was that the lagging had deteriorated to such an extent that it should be removed under the conditions which would be required under the relevant statutes, as if the building were a factory for the purposes of those statutes. A letter written by an engineer in 1985 acting on behalf of the defendants to submit a tender for the work stated:

> Workers must be supplied with appropriate protective clothing and masks. All removal of contaminated and washing facilities must be within the confined area. Workers, when washed, should then move directly to their clean change area.

Despite this, the plaintiff was obliged to continue working in the area and at no stage was informed of the existence of asbestos or the risks attached to asbestos dust.

The decision was appealed by the defendants.

Keane C.J. held that:

> I am, accordingly, satisfied that the law in this jurisdiction should not be extended by the courts so as to allow the recovery by plaintiffs of damages for psychiatric injury resulting from an irrational fear of contracting a disease because of their negligent exposure to health risks by their employers, where the risk is characterised by their medical advisors as very remote.

Proper Equipment/Safe System

McGann v Manning Construction Ltd [2003] HC is a case in point here.

Facts: the plaintiff had been involved in constructing shuttering as part of renovations that were being carried out. While hammering nails through a wooden frame into a concrete wall a sliver of metal from the top of a nail flew into his left eye, perforating his iris before embedding itself in his eye. The plaintiff had been given directions in relation to the work the previous day. When the accident happened he was not wearing safety glasses. While there was some debate over whether glasses had or had not been issued, in the absence of evidence from the employer on the matter the Court decided on the plaintiff's evidence that there had not been any glasses issued. It accepted that there was an onus on an employer in the circumstances to provide safety equipment to protect employees from such injuries as are reasonably foreseeable. There was also a general duty to instruct employees on safety procedures.

Held: the employer had failed to provide such equipment as was reasonably necessary to protect the plaintiff from injury. There had been a failure to properly instruct the plaintiff on safety procedures. In addition, there had been a failure to properly enforce the wearing of appropriate safety equipment by employees. Contributory negligence was found against the plaintiff in that he had failed to comply with signs in the workplace stating that the wearing of safety equipment was mandatory.

Clabby v Global Windows & An Post [2003] HC

Facts: the plaintiff worked as a postman with An Post. In March 1996, while delivering post to a house, he injured his back. The letter-plate to the house was located at the foot of the door, about 2 in. above ground level. He had a bundle of letters in his hand and his post bag, with the remainder of the post on his right shoulder. He bent down on his hunkers, lifted the letter flap with his left hand and inserted a letter with his right hand. When he began to rise to standing again, he experienced pain in his back. In a case against Global Windows Ltd., the manufacturer, supplier and installer of the front door, it was argued that the company:

- knew, or ought to have known, that the low-lying plate represented a hazard to persons using same;
- failed to have any regard for the health and safety of persons using the letter-plate;
- failed to have any regard to Irish Standard 195/1976 of the IIRS and recommendations regarding safe location of letterboxes;
- failed to have any regard to the recommendations of An Post as to the safe location of letter-plates.

Low-lying letterboxes were recognised by An Post and by postmen as a problem. In fact, since 1966 An Post, and earlier the Department of Posts and Telegraphs, had made efforts to persuade various statutory bodies to regulate the positioning of letter-plates on the grounds that low letter-plates represented a health hazard in terms of potential for causing back injury. A report was commissioned in 1994 and on the basis of that An Post wrote to, amongst others, the Irish Homebuilders Association and the Royal Institute of Architects of Ireland, stating that badly placed letterboxes could have a detrimental effect on the health of delivery staff. In evidence it was clear that the problem was seen as one of lower back injury resulting from repetitive bending. Medical evidence for the plaintiff was that the risk was no different from that involved in picking up a pin from the floor. The more frequently the operation is carried out, the greater the risk. The injury can be avoided, however, by adopting a proper posture.

Held: the plaintiff had been trained in lifting techniques and was advised as to the method of delivery into low-lying letter-plates. The plaintiff had not followed these techniques. It was recommended that postbags should be removed from the shoulder; the plaintiff had not done this. It was also noted that the householder was largely ignored in debate and discussion about the positioning of letter-plates—this was not addressed as an issue in either the Irish or British standards. If the concern was health and safety, the Court suggested one would expect a recommendation that a letterbox be fitted behind letter-plates so as to avoid the necessity of bending down to the floor to collect post. There was no such recommendation. The only concern by a statutory body, in I.S. 195 of 1976, was in relation to the danger of sharp edges on letter-plates and the inconvenience of letter-plates that are too high or too low. No statutory body had taken measures in relation to the positioning of letter-plates. The risk was not one of which the defendant ought reasonably to have been aware. The injury to the plaintiff was caused by the manner in which the plaintiff carried out the delivery of the letter, i.e. his failure to adopt the correct posture by keeping his postbag on his shoulder.

• Legislation

The Safety, Health and Welfare at Work Act 1989 was significant in that it introduced a legal framework for the management of safety and health at workplace level. It also went beyond that local level by addressing the issue at national level. The Act therefore approached the issues at two levels—local and national—placing obligations on those in the workplace, on employers, employees, suppliers, manufacturers and designers, etc., as well as establishing an Authority at national level to enforce those obligations.

Duties on Employers

Section 6 of the 1989 Act states that *'It shall be the duty of every employer to ensure, so far as is reasonably practicable, the safety, health and welfare at work of all his employees'.*

This duty applies with regard to:
- place of work;
- access to and egress from that place;
- the design, provision and maintenance of plant and machinery;
- system of work;
- information, training and supervision;
- provision of protective clothing or equipment, as appropriate;
- emergency plans;
- use of hazardous articles or substances;
- arrangements for the welfare of employees;
- obtaining, where necessary, the services of a competent person.

Duties on Employees

Section 9: places certain duties on all employees. These duties apply with regard to:
- taking reasonable care for their own safety and that of others who may be affected by their actions;

- co-operating with employers to facilitate compliance with the relevant law;
- the correct use of any protective equipment or clothing;
- the prompt reporting of any defects in plant, equipment, place or system of work.

Duties on Other Parties
Section 10: places certain duties on designers, manufacturers, importers and suppliers of any article or substance for use in the workplace.

Section 11: places duties on the designers and those who construct workplaces.

Safety Statements
Section 12: obliges every employer to prepare a written safety statement in which hazards are identified, risks are assessed and the steps necessary to deal with those hazards and risks are set out clearly.

Employee Consultation
Section 13: deals with employer consultation with employees and the issue of representation in relation to safety issues.

Health and Safety Authority
Section 14: establishes the National Authority for Occupational Safety and Health, commonly known as the Health & Safety Authority (HSA). Not only was the Act addressing safety at local level, it was also addressing it at national level. The HSA was charged with enforcement functions as well as the tasks of monitoring the legislation, drawing up codes of practice, undertaking research in the area, providing information and generally fostering a culture of safety. A breach of the Act would constitute a criminal offence and as such the alleged wrongdoer could be prosecuted.

• Safety, Health and Welfare at Work Act 2005
On 22 June 2005 a new Safety, Health and Welfare at Work Act was passed and came into force on 1 September 2005, repealing in its entirety the first Safety, Health and Welfare at Work Act 1989. The 2005 Act represents an expanded version of the earlier 1989 Act, with some significant additions. It sets out the duties of employers, employees and other parties associated with the workplace, such as designers of workplaces and workplace equipment and suppliers of goods for use in the workplace. Enforcement procedures have been strengthened, with significant increases in penalties available. Account is also taken of the developments in Irish society in terms of widening ethnic and cultural diversity and increased lifestyle choices.

The 2005 Act comprises eight parts and seven schedules.

Parts

Part 1   Preliminary and General: definitions, repeals, etc.

Part 2   General Duties: duties of employers, information for employees, emergencies and imminent dangers; general duties of employees and persons in control of places of work; duties of designers, manufacturers, importers and suppliers of articles; duties related to construction work.

Part 3   Protective and preventive measures: hazard identification, risk assessment and health surveillance; Safety Statement.

Part 4   Safety Representation and Safety Consultation.

Part 5   The Health and Safety Authority: functions, membership.

Part 6   Regulations, Codes of Practice and Enforcement: powers of inspectors, enforcement procedures.

Part 7   Offences and penalties.

Part 8   Miscellaneous.

Schedules

Part 2: General Duties of the Employer
Section 8 of the Act, echoing and building significantly on the 1989 Act, sets out the general duties of the employer to employees, be they wholetime, fixed-term or temporary:

> Every employer shall ensure, so far as is reasonably practicable, the safety, health and welfare at work of his or her employees.

Section 2(1) gives a broad definition of the term *employer:*

> *employer*, in relation to an employee-
> (a) means the person with whom the employee has entered into or for whom the employee works under (or, where the employment has ceased, entered into or worked under) a contract of employment,
> (b) includes a person (other than an employee of that person) under whose control and direction an employee works, and
> (c) includes, where appropriate, the successor of the employer or an associated employer of the employer.

What is significant is that where employees move between companies for temporary purposes, the employer who is in control of the working environment is the employer for the purposes of this Act, whether or not s/he is the true employer of the employee in question.

Interestingly, the Act contains the first ever statutory definition of the term *reasonably practicable.* Section 2(6) of Part 1 of the Act states:

> For the purposes of the relevant statutory provisions, 'reasonably practicable', in relation to the duties of an employer, means that an employer has exercised all due care by putting in place the necessary protective and preventive measures, having identified the hazards and assessed the risks to safety and health likely to result in accidents or injury to health at the place of work concerned and where the putting in place of any further measures is grossly disproportionate having regard to the unusual, unforeseeable and exceptional nature of any circumstance or occurrence that may result in an accident at work or injury to health at that place of work.

A case where the term *reasonably practicable* was considered was the Supreme Court case of *Boyle v Marathon Petroleum (Ireland) Ltd* [1999] (Unreported). Here, O'Flaherty J. stated:

> I have no doubt that the onus of proof does rest on the defendants to show that what they did was what was reasonably practicable. I am also of the opinion that this duty is more extensive than the common law duty which devolves on employers to exercise reasonable care in various aspects as regards their employees. It is an obligation to take all practical steps. That seems to me to involve more than that they should respond that they, as employers, did all that was reasonably to be expected of them in that particular situation.

In the instant case it was accepted by the Supreme Court that *reasonably practicable* precautions had been taken where a high-risk situation had been dealt with, but that the measures taken had left a residual low risk. The plaintiff, working on an offshore gas platform, had hit his head against a girder hanging from a mezzanine floor. The plaintiff was required to clean under the floor approximately four to five times a year. The mezzanine floor was not part of the original structure, but had been installed following complaints from maintenance workers that the absence of the floor put their safety at serious risk. The maintenance workers used the mezzanine on a daily basis.

In the *Annotated Legislation Series* (Round Hall, Safety, Health and Welfare at Work Act 2005), Byrne notes the enforcement proceedings initiated by the European Commission against the UK and Ireland for the continued use of *reasonably practicable* in domestic legislation. The term was not used in the 1989 Framework Directive on Safety at Work (Directive 89/391/EEC) and there was the perception that its use constituted a watering-down of the duty concerned. This is not to suggest that the standard desired was absolute liability. As Byrne points out, Art 5.4 of the Framework Directive seems to envisage a *reasonably practicable* test. Article 5.4 states:

> This Directive shall not restrict the option of the Member States to provide for the exclusion or the limitation of employers' responsibility where occurrences are due to unusual and unforeseeable circumstances, beyond the employers' control, or to exceptional events, the consequences of which could not have been avoided despite the exercise of all due care.

As enforcement proceedings against Ireland (but not the UK) have since been dropped, it would appear that the statutory definition adopted in the 2005 Act is in compliance with Art 5.4 of the Framework Directive.

As in the 1989 Act, a workplace is quite broadly defined and includes:

> Section 2 (1)   any, or any part of any, place (whether or not within or forming part of a building or structure), land or other location at, in, upon or near which, work is carried on whether occasionally or otherwise and in particular includes –
> (a) in relation to an extractive industry including exploration activity, the whole area intended to house workstations to which employees have access for the purpose of their work relating to the immediate and ancillary activities and installations of, as appropriate-
>> (i) the surface or, as the case may be, underground extractive industry, including overburden dumps and other tips and any accommodation that is provided and, in the case of the underground extractive industry, any working area,
>> (ii) the extractive industry through drilling onshore including any accommodation that is provided, and
>> (iii) the extractive industry through drilling offshore, including any accommodation that is provided,
> (b) a tent, trailer, temporary structure or moveable structure, and
> (c) a vehicle, vessel or aircraft.

• Part 2

As with the 1989 Act and indeed similar legislation in other jurisdictions, the duty placed on an employer is not an unlimited one. The employer is not an insurer. Similar to the common law position, but arguably going beyond it in the 2005 Act, in the circumstances the employer is obliged to act as a prudent employer should. Clearly employers need to examine the environment in which their employees work in order to meet this obligation. What are the hazards in the workplace? What levels of risk are the employees exposed to in the course of their work? Have appropriate steps been taken to deal with these matters? Proportionality is crucial to this question.

> S8 (1)   Every employer shall ensure, so far as is reasonably practicable, the safety, health and welfare at work of his or her employees.
>
> S8(2) ... the employer's duty extends, in particular, to the following:
>
> (a) managing and conducting work activities in such a way as to ensure, so far as is reasonably practicable, the safety, health and welfare at work of his or her employees;
> (b) managing and conducting work activities in such a way as to prevent, so far as is reasonably practicable, any improper conduct or behaviour likely to put the safety, health or welfare at work of his or her employees at risk.

The *managing and conducting of work activities* is a clear shift in focus from the 1989 Act. Clearly the requirement now is that the employer manages and monitors activities on an ongoing basis. This calls for a more integrated approach, where safety is embedded in the culture of the organisation. Putting a safe system in place is not adequate, it must be monitored and revised on an ongoing basis.

Preventing improper behaviour that is likely to put employees at risk not only requires a management and monitoring system but also a means of effectively dealing with such behaviour if it does arise. An employer would need to consider what mechanisms are in place to address bullying or harassment, for example, in addition to what might be construed as less serious examples of improper behaviour. This duty cannot be taken in isolation from the obvious obligation it places on employees or others not to engage carelessly or deliberately in improper behaviour likely to cause injury to others.

Section 8: continues with outlining the employer's duties as follows:

• ensuring a safe place of work, including the design and maintenance;
• safe access to and egress from;

- safe plant and machinery;
- prevention of risk relating to any article, substance, vibration, exposure to noise, ionising or other radiations or any other physical agent;
- providing appropriately planned, organised, performed, maintained and revised systems of work;
- providing and maintaining facilities and arrangements for the welfare of employees;
- providing necessary information, instruction, training and supervision;
- identifying hazards, assessing risks in a safety statement and implementing the measures necessary for protection of the employees;
- providing and maintaining suitable protective clothing and equipment where risks cannot be eliminated;
- emergency/evacuation plans;
- reporting accidents;
- obtaining, where necessary, the services of a competent person for the purposes of ensuring the safety, health and welfare of employees.

Note: s 8(3) states that the duty applies not just to wholetime employees but to anyone employed on a fixed-term or temporary basis.

Section 9: is concerned with the type of information that must be provided by an employer to employees in relation to health, safety and welfare in the workplace. *Per* s 9(a) the information must be given '*in a form, manner and, as appropriate, language that is reasonably likely to be understood by the employees concerned*'.

With increasing multiculturalism in the workplace, particular consideration must be given to necessary and appropriate methods chosen to communicate this information effectively. This may also impact on how information is communicated to employees who are sight-impaired or to employees with literacy difficulties. It would also concern employees from other companies engaged in work activities temporarily in the workplace.

The information supplied must include the following:

> S9(b):
> (i) the hazards to safety, health and welfare and the risks identified in the risk assessment,
> (ii) the protective and preventive measures to be taken concerning safety, health and welfare at work under the relevant statutory provisions in respect of the place of work and each specific task to be performed at the place of work, and
> (iii) the name(s) of the persons designated under section 11 and of safety representatives selected under section 25, if any.

Section 11: refers to persons responsible for first aid, evacuation procedures, etc.

Section 10: outlines the instruction, training and supervision systems that must be put in place for employees in relation to their safety, health and welfare. Specifically:

- it must be in a form and manner that is reasonably likely to be understood;
- employees must receive, where appropriate, time off work for adequate safety, health and welfare training without loss of remuneration;
- an employee's capabilities must be taken into account;
- employees with particular sensitivities must be protected against the dangers that affect them specifically;
- training must adapt to new or changed risks posed to safety, health and welfare;
- training shall take place on recruitment, transfer, where a new task is assigned, or when new equipment, systems of work or new technology is introduced.

Section 11: deals with emergencies and serious and imminent dangers in the workplace. Under this section an employer must prepare, and revise as necessary, adequate plans and procedures to be followed in the case of an emergency or serious threat to safety. This relates to first aid, fire-fighting and the evacuation of anyone present in the workplace, as well as arranging necessary contacts with emergency services. It also states that employers should designate employees who will implement the plans and ensure that these employees are trained adequately to do so. Where there is an emergency or imminent danger, an employer is obliged to inform all employees of the risks and the steps to be taken to protect themselves. This may also require enabling the employees to leave the area of danger and restricting access to such areas to those who have received appropriate instruction.

Section 12: obliges an employer to again *manage and conduct* his/her undertaking in such a way as to ensure, so far as is reasonably practicable, that in the course of the work being carried out, individuals at the place of work (not being employees) are not exposed to risks to their safety, health or welfare.

Duties of Employees
Section 13 (see Chapter 2): sets out the duties the Act places on employees, namely that an employee must:
- comply with relevant statutory provisions and take reasonable care for his/her safety, health and welfare and that of any other person who may be affected by his/her acts or omissions at work;
- ensure s/he is not under the influence of any intoxicant to the extent that safety, health or welfare is compromised;
- submit to appropriate, reasonable and proportionate tests for intoxicants;

- co-operate with the employer or others to enable compliance with relevant statutory provision;
- not engage in improper behaviour likely to endanger others;
- attend safety training;
- make correct use of any substance or article provided for the protection of his/her safety, health and welfare;
- report dangers posed to the health, safety and welfare of employees, including works being carried out, defects in the place or system of work, articles or substances that might endanger lives and any infringements of relevant statutory provisions.

Employees should not put themselves in a position where they might be a danger to themselves and to others in the workplace. As it is not always the case that employees may realise that there might be safety issues, employers should have policies in place to cover such possibilities, particularly in high-risk occupations. A mandatory reporting policy should be considered by such employers, obliging employees to notify the employer that they have suffered a traumatic event. A well-known Irish low-cost airline introduced a policy making it mandatory for every pilot to advise the company if s/he suffered a bereavement in the family, in which case s/he would receive compassionate leave. This followed a safety incident where a pilot suffered a breakdown in the cockpit days after the tragic death of one of his children.

A significant addition to the duties of employees under the 2005 Act is the duty to submit to appropriate, reasonable and proportionate tests for intoxicants. For the employer it will be imperative that the correct balance be achieved between ensuring safety in the workplace and respecting the personal rights of employees. This will very much be determined by the nature of the work in which the employee is engaged and by the likely risk the employee might pose. An administrator might not pose the same risk to himself, herself or others as a pilot, a driver or a person operating machinery. Given recent developments in case law, disability law may also have an impact because if the intoxication is caused by alcoholism, this might affect the way in which an employer could deal with the issue within the law.

Section 14: places a general obligation on any person in a workplace not to misuse, damage or interfere with anything provided for the protection of safety, health and welfare of persons at work.

Section 15: is concerned with the duties of persons in control of a non-domestic place of work towards persons working who are not their employees. It extends to means of access or egress and to any articles or substances used in that workplace. The duty requires that there should not be a risk to safety or health, so far as is reasonably practicable.

Section 16: goes beyond the employer and the employee and sets out the duties imposed on other persons connected to a workplace. In this context other persons include a person who designs, manufactures, imports or supplies any article for use at work. These persons must:

- ensure, insofar as is reasonably practicable, that the article designed and constructed is safe when used properly;
- ensure compliance with relevant statutory provisions and with the provisions of any relevant enactment implementing any relevant directive of the European Communities;
- ensure appropriate levels of testing and examination;
- provide adequate information to the end user and revise as appropriate;
- carry out any necessary research to eliminate or minimise any risks to safety, health and welfare;
- where assembling or installing is concerned, ensure proper practices.

Section 17: relates to the construction of workplaces. A person who commissions or procures a project for construction work shall appoint, in writing, a competent person to ensure the safety of the design, the construction and the subsequent maintenance and that statutory provisions are complied with. The designer and the person undertaking the construction have the same statutory obligations.

Part 3: Local Implementation of the Act
Competent Person
Section 18: sets out the mechanism by which protective and preventive measures are to be achieved by an employer for the purpose of complying with the Act. The employer must appoint one or more competent person/s, a competent person under the Act being someone who possesses sufficient training, experience and knowledge appropriate to the nature of the work to be undertaken. The time allocated to such a person to carry out his/her duties must be adequate, having regard to the size of the workplace and the nature of the risks to which employees are exposed.

Section 18(4): provides that, where possible, an employer should make an internal appointment.

An employer is obliged to provide such person/s with certain information, which must include:
- factors, known or suspected, that affect safety, health and welfare of employees;
- risks to the above and measures necessary to prevent or protect from same;
- evacuation procedures;
- reasonable information about fixed-term or temporary employees, as is necessary.

Hazard Identification and Risk Assessment

Under s 19 the employer must identify the hazards in the workplace that are under his/her control and assess the risks posed to the safety, health and welfare of the employees by those hazards. This risk assessment must be in written form. Special mention must be made where there is a particular risk to any single employee or group of employees. For example, pregnant employees would be one such category of employee to bear in mind here. Employers should note that in the Act this is not a once-off activity and must be reviewed as the need arises as, for example, when there has been a significant change to the issues to which it related or where it is believed the assessment is no longer valid. It should also be noted that the duties cover persons other than his/her employees.

A *hazard* may be defined as anything with the potential to cause harm. While the term is not actually defined in the Act, in its *Short Guide to the Safety, Health and Welfare at Work Act 2005* the HSA provides a non-exhaustive checklist of typical workplace hazards in a broad range of employments, and includes the following as useful guidance:

- slips, trips and falls;
- falls of persons from a height;
- falls of material from a height;
- hazards from plant and machinery;
- hazards associated with the manual handling of loads;
- fire and explosion;
- the use of hazardous substances;
- exposure to harmful levels of noise, radiation, vibration;
- unsuitable lighting levels in work areas;
- use of visual display screens;
- human factors, such as violence to staff members, bullying in the workplace or stress.

A *risk* may be defined as the likelihood of harm occurring and the severity of the consequences if it does. A risk may range in severity from being a high risk, a medium risk or a low risk. Categorising the risk is essential to the task of prioritising the measures necessary to ensure the proper management of safety, health and welfare in the workplace. Having identified the hazards and assessed the associated risks, the employer must at this stage select the appropriate measures to eliminate the hazards or, where that is not possible, to minimise the risks.

Safety Statement

Section 20: provides that, following on from the risk assessment and hazard identification exercise, an employer must have a written safety statement. This statement specifies how safety, health and welfare will be secured and managed. Specifically this statement must set out:

- the hazards identified in the workplace and the risks posed by them;
- the measures in place to deal with these;
- emergency plans;
- duties of employees regarding safety, health and welfare, including the requirement to co-operate with the employer and others with designated roles of responsibility in matters relating to safety, health and welfare;
- the names of those with responsibility for safety matters, safety representatives and safety committee;
- procedures for appointing safety representatives;
- arrangements for consultation with employees and safety representatives.

The safety statement must be presented in a form that is reasonably likely to be understood. It must be brought to the attention of employees, so prominent display and easy accessibility are crucial. With a multicultural workforce special consideration must be given to language levels and it might be more appropriate to produce the statement in a number of languages reflecting the ethnic backgrounds of the workforce. It should be presented at least annually and at times when it has been amended. It must be reviewed and amended as appropriate. Employers must also bring the safety statement to the attention of new employees and to other persons at the place of work who may be exposed to any specific danger to which the safety statement refers.

Only employers of three or fewer employees are exempt from the requirement to have an up-to-date safety statement. They are in compliance with the Act in this regard so long as they observe the provisions of a Code of Practice.

Health Surveillance
Section 22: requires the employer to provide for health surveillance of his/her employees appropriate to the risks identified in the risk assessment:

> S2(1): health surveillance means the periodic review, for the purpose of protecting health and preventing occupationally related disease, of the health of employees, so that any adverse variations in their health that may be related to working conditions are identified as early as possible.

Medical Assessments
Section 23: allows an employer to require an employee to undergo a medical assessment of their fitness by a registered medical practitioner nominated by the employer where the work performed gives rise to serious risks to the safety, health and welfare of persons at work.

If such class of employee becomes aware that s/he is suffering from any disease or physical or mental impairment that would be likely to cause him/her to expose himself/herself or another person to danger or risk should s/he perform a work activity, the employer must be notified immediately either directly or through a medical practitioner. Where an employer receives such notification, *'he or she shall immediately take appropriate action to comply with his or her general duties'.*

Joint Safety and Health Agreements

Section 24: allows for 'joint safety and health agreements' to be entered into by trade unions and employers. Such agreements must be approved by the governing Authority:

> A trade union of employees, representing a class or classes of employees, and a trade union of employers may-
> (a) enter into or vary an agreement (in this Act referred to as a joint safety and health agreement) providing practical guidance to the employees and employers with respect to safety, health and welfare at work including the requirements of the relevant statutory provisions.

Part 4: Safety Representatives

Section 25 gives employees the right to select from their number a Safety Representative or, with their employer's agreement, more than one to represent them in consultations with the employer on issues of safety, health and welfare at the workplace. The Safety Representative has particular powers and responsibilities under the Act, which allows him/her to:

- inspect the workplace in the event of an accident or imminent danger;
- investigate accidents and dangerous occurrences;
- investigate employee complaints after giving reasonable notice to the employer;
- accompany Authority inspectors on routine inspections or, at their discretion, conduct inspections investigating an accident;
- make representations to the employer or Authority inspectors on any matter relating to safety, health and welfare in the workplace;
- receive advice and information from inspectors on matters relating to safety, health and welfare;
- agree the frequency of inspections to be carried out, having regard to the nature and extent of hazards in that particular workplace.

An employer must consider any representations made by the Safety Representative and, insofar as is reasonably practicable, act upon them.

The Safety Representative must be given reasonable time off work, without loss of pay, to discharge his/her functions and to ensure his/her skills remain current through appropriate ongoing training.

Consultation

Section 26: is concerned with employee consultation and employees' involvement in discussions in all matters relating to health and safety at work. Consultation processes may take place through the establishing of a Safety Committee, where the employer agrees to such a body being formed.

Part 5: The Authority

Section 32: is concerned with the Health & Safety Authority (HSA), referred to in the Act as 'the Authority'. Set up under the 1989 Act, the HSA continues under the 2005 Act but with an expanded role. The HSA is a body corporate in law with perpetual succession, with the right to sue and to be sued and, with ministerial approval, enjoys the right to acquire, hold and dispose of land or other property.

Section 34: sets out the general functions of the Authority as being to:
- promote the prevention of accidents and personal injury;
- promote safety education and training;
- facilitate the enforcement of relevant statutory provisions;
- monitor and make recommendations to the Minister regarding implementation and compliance with relevant statutory provisions and best practice;
- provide information and advice on safety, health and welfare;
- engage in or facilitate research;
- prepare a strategy statement for the following three-year period;
- prepare an annual work programme;
- prepare an annual report for the Minister;
- perform any additional functions conferred on it by ministerial order.

Section 37: provides that the Authority be composed of a chairperson and eleven ordinary members, who are appointed by the Minister. The ordinary members comprise:
- three persons nominated by employees' organisations;
- three persons nominated by employers' organisations;
- five persons considered appropriate by the Minister, including one person from the Department of Enterprise, Trade and Employment, under which the Authority operates.

Section 38: gives the Authority the power to establish advisory committees from time to time to advise it in relation to any of its functions.

Section 36: gives the Authority the power to set up subsidiaries to carry out some of its functions, with the exception of its enforcement responsibilities.

Section 40: gives the Authority the power, if it considers it necessary, to at any time engage consultants or advisors.

Part 6: Regulations, Codes of Practice and Enforcement Procedures

Section 57: obliges the Authority to keep under review the relevant statutory provisions, to submit proposals to the Minister it considers appropriate and to assist in the preparation of draft legislation.

Section 58: gives power to the Minister for Enterprise, Trade and Employment to make regulations for any matter referred to in the Act, or generally for the purposes of giving full effect to the Act or in respect of any of the matters set out in Schedule 7.

Section 60: empowers the Authority to draft codes of practice, *'For the purpose of providing practical guidance to employers, employees and any other persons to whom this Act applies with respect to safety, health and welfare at work'*. The consent of the Minister is required before such codes may be published.

The Authority has the responsibility for enforcing the Act and will do this in a number of ways.

Section 64: provides that the first line of enforcement rests with the inspectorate. The Authority appoints inspectors to effect compliance with the Act. To this end, the inspectors are granted the following powers:

- at any time enter any place s/he reasonably believes to be a workplace and search and examine any activity, article, substance, record or remove and retain same to ascertain compliance with the relevant statutory provisions;
- order the amendment of the safety statement;
- on foot of a written notice, summon the employer, employee, owner or person in charge to give any information reasonably required;
- take measurements, photographs or recordings;
- where appropriate, install monitoring equipment;
- test or have tested or analysed any article or substance s/he reasonably considers to be necessary;
- take atmospheric samples.

When an inspector enters upon a premises it must be with the consent of the occupier or, failing that, must be on foot of a District Court warrant. An inspector may be accompanied by a member of An Garda Síochána, if necessary.

Improvement Plan

Section 65: provides that where an inspector believes there is a likely risk to safety, health or welfare, s/he may issue the employer concerned with a written direction requesting an Improvement Plan, a copy of which must be given to the safety representative. The Plan, which specifies the activity causing the risk and the remedial action required, must be submitted within one month.

Improvement Notice

Section 66: provides that the next possible stage in enforcement is an Improvement Notice. This is issued by an inspector where s/he believes there has been an infringement of the law or where a direction for an Improvement Plan has not been complied with. It sets out the contravention in question, the remedy, the means of appeal and it is signed and dated by the inspector. A copy must be given to the Safety Representative. Such notice may be appealed to the District Court within fourteen days of its issue.

In cases of a likely risk of serious injury, an inspector may issue a written notice, called a Prohibition Notice, to the person presumed to be in control of the offending activity. This notice specifies the activity, states the reason for the inspector's opinion and prohibits the activity in question. Anyone whose work is affected by the notice must be informed and the notice must be displayed prominently. Such notices are effective upon receipt and may only be appealed to the District Court. In such case, the notice stands until the appeal is decided upon by the Court. If an inspector is satisfied that the risk no longer exists, s/he may withdraw the notice at any time, in writing. An inspector may take contraventions of Prohibitions Notices to the High Court. This may be *Ex parte* in that the alleged wrongdoer will not be informed beforehand of the proceedings against him/her.

In addition to the inspectors' role in enforcement, the Authority may direct its staff, or any other competent person, to carry out investigations or special reports as it sees fit (s 70). Particular reference is made here to accidents, personal injuries, or *'any other matter related to the general purposes of the Act'*. In the case of air, rail or marine accidents, ministerial consent will be required for such action (s 70.1.a, b, c).

High Court Injunctions

Where the risk to safety is considered to be so serious that use of the workplace should be immediately restricted or prohibited, the HSA, or an approved person, may approach the High Court for an order so restricting or prohibiting. Again this may be *ex parte*, meaning the alleged offender may not be forewarned of the proceedings against him/her. Failure to comply with such an order from the Court constitutes contempt and brings serious consequences, including sequestering of assets and possible incarceration.

The penalties for contraventions of the Act are also quite heavy. For summary convictions or minor infringements the penalty is a fine of €3,000 and/or imprisonment for a period not exceeding six months. For more serious infringements and for indictable offences the penalty is a fine not exceeding €3,000,000 and/or a term of imprisonment not exceeding two years. The Act also introduced on-the-spot fines of €1,000. Furthermore, costs of the court proceedings, of the investigation by the HSA and any other costs arising may have to be borne by the wrongdoer.

> S78(4): where a person is convicted of an offence under the relevant statutory provisions in proceedings brought by the Authority ... the court shall, unless it is satisfied that there are special and substantial reasons for not so doing, order the person to pay to the Authority ... the costs and expenses measured by the court, incurred by the Authority ... in relation to the investigation, detection and prosecution of the offence including costs and expenses incurred in the taking of samples, the carrying out of tests, examinations and analyses and in respect of the remuneration and other expenses of employees or of consultants and advisers engaged by the Authority ...

Section 80: introduces new liabilities. Individuals, directors or managers as well as the company may be liable under the Act and punished as appropriate:

> Where an offence ... has been committed by an undertaking and the doing of the acts that constituted the offence has been authorised, or consented to by, or is attributable to connivance or neglect on the part of a person, being a director, manager or other similar officer of the undertaking, or a person who purports to act in any such capacity, that person ... shall be guilty of an offence and shall be liable to be ... punished as if he or she were guilty of the first mentioned offence.

There was some disappointment expressed in certain quarters that the Act did not contain a corporate killing offence. The Law Reform Commission Report of 2005 proposed the establishment of a statutory corporate killing offence to be prosecuted on indictment, whereby the acts or omissions of a *high managerial agent* would be treated as those of the company. This would apply on the death of a person where it could be proved that the acts or omissions in question fell far below what could reasonably be expected in the circumstances and constituted a high degree of risk of serious injury and were a contributing cause of death. Such an offence would be defined in terms equivalent to gross negligence manslaughter and would apply to all companies or undertakings.

Section 85: introduces a *name and shame* facility whereby the HSA may publish details of offenders.

A significant departure from the 1989 Act concerns the civil liability exemption. Breaches of the 1989 Act did not give rise to a cause of action in civil proceedings.

Section 60(1)(a) of the 2005 Act removed this exemption, so it is now possible that breaches will attract both a criminal and a civil sanction.

Prosecutions are taken by the Authority or by a prescribed person under the Act.

In addition to protection provided by legislation such as the Safety, Health and Welfare at Work Act 2005, there are further measures in law that may be invoked in the event of an accident or personal injury in the workplace, namely the Common Law Duties of the Employer. These duties are to be found in civil law, in the law of tort. This area of law has a compensatory function in that it provides a method of redress for individuals who have suffered loss in particular circumstances. Unlike legislation, which is preventive in approach in that it lays down standards to be met, the law of tort acts as a remedy when an accident or injury has occurred.

Maternity Protection Acts 1994–2004 and associated Regulations cover certain matters of health, safety and welfare in the workplace for new and expectant mothers. Certain entitlements are provided by these Acts, including:
- time off without pay for maternity leave;
- time off without loss of pay for ante-natal and post-natal care;
- leave where a risk assessment shows that employment of a pregnant or breastfeeding mother is hazardous to the woman's or baby's health;
- rest areas in the workplace.

• Occupiers' Liability Act 1995
The employer should also be aware of his/her obligations under the Occupiers' Liability Act 1995.

Section 1: defines an *occupier* as:

> … a person exercising such control over the state of the premises that it is reasonable to impose upon that person a duty towards an entrant in respect of a particular danger thereon.

Premises are defined as including:

> Land, water and any fixed or moveable structures thereon and also includes vessels, vehicles, trains, aircraft and other means of transport.

Under this Act the occupier of a premises has certain duties in relation to the safety of persons coming onto a premises. These duties vary depending on the nature of the entrant, be it a visitor, a recreational user or a trespasser.

The Public Health (Tobacco) Acts 2002, 2004 provide that most enclosed places of work are smoke-free. The ban on smoking in the workplace was introduced as a health and safety measure and should also be considered within the context of the Safety, Health and Welfare at Work Act 2005. As an employer is obliged to ensure the health, safety and welfare of all employees insofar as is reasonably practicable, employees should expect that they will not be exposed to an unsafe working environment.

Section 47 of the 2002 Act allowed the Minister for Health and Children to prohibit or restrict the smoking of tobacco products in a place of work.

Section 16 of the 2004 Act, in amending s 47, went much further. This section prohibited the smoking of a tobacco product in a specified place. A *specified place* is defined as:

(a) a place of work,
(b) an aircraft, train, ship or other vessel, public service vehicle, or a vehicle used for the carriage of members of the public for reward other than a public service vehicle, insofar as it is a place of work,
(c) a health premises, insofar as it is a place of work,
(d) a hospital that is not a health premises, insofar as its is a place of work,
(e) a school or college, insofar as it is a place of work,
(f) a building to which the public has access, either as of right or with the permission of the owner or occupier of the building, and which belongs to, or is in the occupation of ... the State, a Minister ... the Commissioners of Public Works, or a body established by or under an Act,
(g) a cinema, theatre, concert hall or other place normally used for indoor public entertainment, insofar as it is a place of work,
(h) a licensed premises, insofar as it is a place of work,
(i) a registered club, insofar as it is a place of work.

A *place of work* is as defined in the Safety, Health and Welfare at Work Act 2005 and is therefore quite broad. There was considerable discussion as to whether certain workplaces should be exempted, particularly those which act as permanent residences for sections of the community, namely prisons and psychiatric hospitals. As a result there is a large number of exceptions listed in the Acts. Certain places are exempt from this provision, including:

(a) a dwelling;
(b) a prison;
(c) a place or premises or part thereof that is wholly uncovered;

    (d) an outdoor part of a place or premises that is covered provided that not more than 50 per cent of the perimeter is surrounded by walls or similar structure (inclusive of doors, windows);

    (e) a nursing home;

    (f) a hospice;

    (g) a psychiatric hospital or the Central Mental Hospital;

    (h) a bedroom in an hotel or Bed & Breakfast or any other premises where sleeping accommodation is offered to members of the public;

    (i) charitable accommodation.

Where smoking is prohibited, signs must be displayed at all times indicating clearly that smoking is prohibited on those premises and each sign must display the name of the occupier concerned and the name of the person to whom complaints may be made if there are breaches of the ban.

There is no obligation on an employer to provide an outside smoking area.

In the case of employees, breaches of the Act should be regarded as a disciplinary matter and treated accordingly. It is important for employers to have policies in place to ensure compliance with the legislation. Non-compliance with the Acts could be viewed as exposing other employees to an unsafe working environment. Such policies would have to be communicated clearly to employees and to any other persons visiting the workplace. In addition to good signage, the policy should form part of the employees' handbook. Smokers' assistance programmes could also be introduced.

Honeywell International Technologies v Hartery UD 1090/2005 January 2007

    Facts: in December the claimant was caught smoking while working at a particular oven in a secluded part of the factory during the night shift. When he appeared for duty the following night, he was sent home. He was sent a letter of dismissal on 5 January. Following the introduction of the Public Health (Tobacco) Acts the factory was designated a non-smoking area and employees were given permission to smoke in a smoking hut in the car park. This was the only place where smoking was permitted.

Held: the dismissal was deemed to be disproportionate to the offence committed and also to be inconsistent with regard to two previous employees who had received lesser sanctions for similar matters. Those employees had received written warnings. The EAT also stated that there should have been an agreement drawn up making clear to all members of staff the disciplinary procedure for smoking within the workplace. The claimant was awarded €11,000 in compensation.

Where employers take disciplinary action against employees the employees are entitled to fair procedures. In the case of dismissal, protection is afforded under the Unfair Dismissals Acts 1997–2001. Where an employer does not have specific disciplinary procedures in place the Labour Relations Commission's code of practice on disciplinary procedures gives useful guidance.

Collins v Tesco Ireland Ltd [EAT 2006]

Facts: the claimant, a night-shift manager, and a security officer were in the canteen at 2.00am when another employee began to smoke. The employee was not asked by the manager to stop smoking, though should have been, but was requested to so do by the security officer. He ignored the request and moved to a window. The incident was reported by the security officer, but not by the claimant. The claimant had asked the security officer not to report it. Following the reporting of the incident the personnel manager had a meeting with the claimant and suspended him, on full pay, for one week.

An investigation was held one week later, during which the claimant admitted that he had allowed the employee in question to smoke on previous occasions. In advance of a third meeting with the claimant the personnel manager met with the store manager and the employee who had been smoking. The following day the store manager telephoned the claimant and dismissed him. A few days later a letter of dismissal was sent to the claimant. He appealed this decision internally, but was advised that the dismissal for gross misconduct was upheld.

Held: the EAT held that the claimant was dismissed because he *wilfully allowed* an employee to smoke in the canteen. However, the Tribunal found against the employer for a number of reasons, principally concerned with the procedures used to deal with the matter. The claimant was not made aware of the fact that the third meeting was a disciplinary meeting that could have led to dismissal. He was not given sufficient prior notice and the fairness of the internal appeals procedure could not be ascertained. The Tribunal also found that the dismissal was disproportionate.

The claimant was awarded €27,000. The award could have been higher but for the fact that the claimant had not mitigated his loss by attempting to seek suitable alternative employment after the dismissal.

Employers, occupiers of premises and employees should be cognisant of the possible impact of the Litter Pollution Act 1997. Cigarette butts strewn outside public places constitute a clear breach of the Act, therefore suitable receptacles should be provided at entrances of buildings to prevent littering. Section 3(1) of the Act states that *'no person shall deposit any substance or object so as to create litter in a public place or in any place that is visible to any extent from a public place'.*

• Safety, Health and Welfare at Work (General Applications) Regulations 2007

These Regulations, which came into operation in November 2007, update the 1993 General Application Regulations and provide details of essential occupational safety, health and welfare requirements. As with the 2005 Act, the Regulations apply to all workplaces. The Regulations set out requirements in relation to the following:

Part 2: Workplace
- Structural stability, ventilation, room temperature, lighting, floors, walls, ceilings, windows, doors, emergency exits, room dimensions;
- fire detection and fire-fighting;
- rest rooms, sanitary and washing facilities;
- rest rooms for pregnant, post-natal and breastfeeding employees.

Work Equipment
- Properly installed and located equipment suitable for the work;
- proper maintenance, protective guards;
- information on the conditions of use, risks;
- inspections, testing and examination;
- mobile equipment, lifting operations, connection to energy sources.

Personal Protective Equipment
- Provision of equipment;
- assessment and maintenance;
- training, information.

Manual Handling of Loads
- The duty to take appropriate organisational measures to avoid the need for the manual handling of loads or, where the need cannot be avoided, to reduce the risks to employees.

VDUs
- Ensure that the general use of the equipment is not a source of risk for the employee;
- perform an analysis of the workstation to evaluate the health and safety conditions, particularly as regards risks to eyesight;
- provision of eye tests at regular intervals and corrective appliances;
- Schedule 4 sets out minimum requirements for all display screen equipment, with particular reference to display screen, keyboard (shall have matt surface to avoid reflective glare), work surface, chair (shall be adjustable in both height and tilt), environment (space, lighting, radiation, heat).

Part 3: Electricity
- Ensure that all electrical equipment is designed, installed, maintained, protected and used so as to prevent danger;
- protection against electric shock, fencing of outdoor equipment, overhead lines and underground cables.

Part 4: Work at Height
- Organisation, planning and risk assessment of work at height;
- protection of places of work at height, stability of supporting structures, guard-rails, personal fall protection systems;
- scaffolding of good design and construction, falling objects.

Part 5: Physical Agents
- Control of noise at work, prevention of exposure to noise above level of 85dB (A), personal protection, health surveillance;
- control of vibration at work, exposure limits, assessment of risk.

Part 6: Sensitive Risk Group
- Protection of children (under 16) and young persons (16–18 years of age);
- risk assessment, circumstances prohibiting employment of a child or young person;
- protection of pregnant, post-natal and breastfeeding employees;
- night work and shift work, assessment of risks attaching to such work.

Part 7: Safety Signs and First-Aid
- Provision of signs, information and instruction;
- provision of suitably marked and easily accessible first-aid equipment;
- adequate and appropriate provision of first-aiders, first-aid rooms.

Part 8: Explosive Atmospheres
- Risk assessment, provision of protection, training.

In addition to the 2007 Regulations there is a range of Regulations specific to certain work activities and areas. These include:

- Safety, Health and Welfare at Work (Control of Vibration) Regulations 2006;
- Safety, Health and Welfare at Work (Control of Noise at Work) Regulations 2006;
- Safety, Health and Welfare at Work (Exposure to Asbestos) Regulations 2006;
- Safety, Health and Welfare at Work (Construction) Regulations 2006.

The Organisation of Working Time Act 1997
This Act deals with a range of matters relating to the organisation of working time, conditions of employment and health and safety of workers. The Act

provided for the implementation of Directive 93/104/EC and is concerned with rest periods, weekly working hours, nightly working hours and entitlements to annual leave. It provides for the assessment of the safety and health risks attaching to the work of night workers.

Maximum number of hours permitted to work
Section 11: provides for daily rest periods of not less than eleven consecutive hours in each twenty-four-hour period.

Section 15: places a limit of an average of forty-eight hours that a person may work in a week. That average can be calculated over a period that does not generally exceed four months.

Section 19: sets out the entitlement to annual leave; currently it is four weeks. This will include an unbroken period of two weeks where the employee has worked for eight or more months in a leave year.

Section 20: provides that the employer shall determine the times at which annual leave is granted to an employee. Certain issues must be taken into account by the employer in this regard, such as the employee's family/work balance and employee consultation.

chapter 5

BULLYING/HARASSMENT

> **This chapter will examine the following areas:**
> - bullying;
> - harassment;
> - sexual harassment;
> - stress.

For some time now bullying has been recognised, in Ireland as elsewhere, as a significant issue in the workplace. Since the 1990s workplace bullying has been the subject of growing academic and Government interest. There has also been media interest, with some very high-profile cases being reported, a number of which will be examined in this chapter.

In Ireland the importance of addressing workplace bullying has been recognised by the Government with the establishment of the Taskforce on the Prevention of Workplace Bullying in 1999 and the Expert Advisory Group on Workplace Bullying in 2004. Central to the work of these bodies are two commissioned surveys conducted by the Economic and Social Research Institute (ESRI) on the issue of bullying in the workplace, the first of which took place in 2001 and the latest in 2007.

The 2007 survey was designed to ascertain the incidence, correlates and characteristics of bullying in workplaces in Ireland. The survey provided this definition of *bullying*:

> … repeated inappropriate behaviour, direct or indirect, whether verbal, physical or otherwise, conducted by one or more persons against another or others, at the place of work and/or in the course of employment, which could reasonably be regarded as undermining the individual's right to dignity at work. An isolated incident of the behaviour described in this definition may be an affront to dignity at work but is not considered to be bullying.

There is no statutory definition of bullying.

The Code of Practice for Employers and Employees on the Prevention and Resolution of Bullying at Work, produced by the Health and Safety Authority in

2007, sets out a pattern of behaviours that, in its view, constitute bullying, including:
- exclusion with negative consequences;
- verbal abuse or insults;
- being treated less favourably than colleagues;
- intrusion, including pestering, spying or stalking;
- menacing behaviour, intimidation and aggression;
- undermining behaviour;
- excessive monitoring of work;
- humiliation;
- withholding work-related information;
- repeatedly manipulating a person's job content and targets;
- scapegoating/blaming for matters beyond one's control.

Taking the ESRI 2007 survey as the most recent exploration of the issue, a number of findings are noteworthy:
- 7.9 per cent of those at work reported that they had experienced bullying in the workplace in the previous six months. This is slightly increased from the 2001 figure of 7 per cent, but remains lower than the European average, which is reported at 9 per cent;
- women are more at risk of bullying. Less than 6 per cent of men reported bullying in 2007 compared to almost 11 per cent amongst women;
- those with higher levels of educational attainment are more likely to report experiencing bullying in the workplace;
- the sectors with the highest rates of bullying are Education, Public Administration, Health and Social Work and Transport and Communications, with workers in Education and Public Administration being particularly at risk;
- the incidence rate in the public sector is higher than in the private sector;
- bullying is not a top-down, employer-on-employee activity. Organisations are more likely to report that bullying by colleagues and by clients is a problem, rather than bullying by a manager.
  In the public sector, for example:
  - bullying by colleagues—39 per cent,
  - bullying by clients—35.2 per cent,
  - bullying by subordinates—25.8 per cent,
  - bullying by managers—18.6 per cent;
- age has no statistically significant effect on the probability of being bullied;
- the larger the organisation, the greater the prevalence of bullying—10.9 per cent occurrence in large organisations compared with 4.5 per cent in very small organisations with less than five employees;
- workers in organisations undergoing change are more likely to experience bullying;
- there is a strong relationship between employment contract and incidence

rate, with 7.6 per cent in permanent positions experiencing bullying, 9 per cent on temporary contracts, rising to nearly 14 per cent for those on casual contracts;

- 15 per cent of those who experienced bullying left their jobs as a result;
- public sector organisations are more likely to have a formal policy on workplace bullying operating in their organisations than those in the private sector, with 81.9 per cent in the public sector reporting having a formal policy as opposed to 36.9 per cent in the private sector.

Bullying is a health and safety issue.

• Legal Situation
2007 Code of Practice
On 1 May 2007 a Code of Practice was introduced into law under s 60 of the Safety, Health and Welfare at Work Act 2005 entitled *Code of Practice for Employers and Employees on the Prevention and Resolution of Workplace Bullying*. This Code of Practice replaces the 2002 Code, which was brought about by the 1989 Act.

It is a Code for both employers and employees and provides practical guidance for employers arising from their ongoing duties under s 8 of the 2005 Act.

Section 8 concerns the employer's duty regarding:

> managing and conducting work activities in such a way as to prevent, so far as is reasonably practicable, any improper conduct or behaviour likely to put the safety, health and welfare at work of his or her employees at risk.

There is an obligation on every employer to ensure, *insofar as is reasonably practicable*, the safety, health and welfare at work of his/her employees.

The Code, introduced under the Act, also concerns the duties of employees, under s 13(1)(e) of the Act, '*not to engage in improper conduct or behaviour that is likely to endanger his or her own safety, health and welfare at work or that of any other person*'.

Legal Status
Failing to follow the Code is not an offence in itself, but the Code is admissible in evidence in the event of criminal proceedings under s 61 of the 2005 Act.

> S61 (1): Where in proceedings for an offence under this Act relating to an alleged contravention of any requirement or prohibition imposed by or under a relevant statutory provision

being a provision for which a code of practice has been published or approved by the Authority under section 60 at the time of the alleged contravention, subsection (2) shall have effect with respect to that code of practice in relation to those proceedings.

(2) (a) Where a code of practice referred to in subsection (1) appears to the court to give practical guidance as to the observance of the requirement or prohibition alleged to have been contravened, the code of practice shall be admissible in evidence.

(b) Where it is proved that any act or omission of the defendant alleged to constitute the contravention:

(i) is a failure to observe a code of practice referred to in subsection (1), or

(ii) is a compliance with that code of practice, then such failure or compliance is admissible in evidence.

The Code is careful to point out that reasonable and essential disciplinary action in the course of work or actions necessary for the safety, health and welfare of employees would not constitute bullying. It is given clearly that bullying constitutes a pattern of behaviour: a once-off incident does not constitute bullying, although it may be an affront to dignity.

Employees' Rights/Duties under the Code

Section 3.4: addresses the rights and duties of employees. Employees have the right to be treated with dignity and not to have their safety, health or welfare put at risk through bullying by the employer, by fellow employees or by other persons. They have a right of complaint and a right to representation when raising an issue. This section also examines employees' duties. Employees have a duty to respect the rights of the employer and other employees to dignity and respect at work and their right not to have their safety, health and welfare put at risk through bullying.

• Safety Statement

When preparing a Safety Statement under s 20 of the 2005 Act, the employer is obliged to consider whether bullying is likely to be a hazard in the workplace. If it is likely, what are the risks and what preventive measures are necessary?

Bullying Prevention Policy

Measures to prevent bullying would include a formal policy on the issue.

Section 4: states that *'Employers should adopt, implement and monitor a comprehensive, effective and accessible policy on bullying at work'.*

The Code advises that any policy should be arrived at through a consultative process with other parties to the employment relationship, i.e. clients, customers, trade unions or employee representatives, including the Safety Representative or the Safety Committee. The policy document should be written, dated and signed by a person at senior management level. It should be a living document that is updated as appropriate.

The policy should make a clear statement on the employer's commitment to provide a work environment where there is respect, collaboration, openness, safety and equality, where bullying by the employer, employees or non-employees will not be tolerated. It should state that all employees have the right to be treated with respect and dignity at work, while at the same time being obliged to ensure that they themselves refrain from behaviour likely to contribute to bullying. Finally, it should include the proviso that any complaints of bullying will be treated with fairness, sensitivity and in confidence.

Where the alleged bully is concerned, it is important to note that s/he also has certain rights protected by law. S/he must be treated with fairness, sensitivity and the need for confidentiality on behalf of all parties concerned must be respected. It is imperative that natural justice be observed in any investigation of an allegation.

Where there is a finding of bullying after investigation, or where there is a finding that the complaint has been vexatious, the policy should be clear that such findings will be dealt with through a disciplinary procedure. In cases where the bullying is by clients, customers or business contacts, the policy should indicate the likely outcome of termination of contracts, suspension of services or exclusion from a premises or other appropriate sanction.

The Code advises that the policy should describe what is meant by bullying. It should state that protection from bullying extends beyond the place of work to off-site and to work-related social events. The name or job title of the person in the organisation who may be approached by a person wishing to make a complaint should be included in the policy document. That 'contact person' acts as a listener/advisor. S/he would provide the complainant with a copy of the policy and information on steps the complainant may take. The 'contact person' is not an advocate for either side.

Communicating the Policy

Effective communication is essential for the proper implementation of any policy. All employees should be made aware of the policy and should receive updates as they arise. If training is required in order to comply with the policy, it should be provided, particularly for those individuals who have responsibility for its implementation or for responding to complaints. A summary of the policy should be displayed at locations where members of the public, clients and customers attend.

Procedures for Resolving Bullying in the Workplace

The Code outlines two procedures—one informal, the other formal—to be followed in the event of a complaint of bullying being received. Both procedures should be outlined in the Bullying Prevention Policy.

Informal Process

An informal process attempts to resolve the matter informally, with the consent of the parties involved. Ascertaining the facts of the complaint and that they fall within the definition of bullying is the first step. The complaint may be verbal or written, but where verbal a note of the substance of the complaint should be taken by the person designated to deal with it and a copy given to the complainant. The person complained against should have the opportunity to have his/her response established.

The task of resolving the matter should not be taken by the employer or by a person heading up the organisation, but by another senior manager designated to deal with this specific complaint. Training should be in place for those who are engaged with the process at this stage. This person should not be the 'contact person', who is the initial facilitator in the process. If necessary, the services of an outside, independent body should be employed, which may include the Mediation Services of the Labour Relations Commission. This process should identify an agreed method to bring the issue to resolution so that both parties can return to a harmonious workplace environment. If the behaviour complained of does not constitute bullying, an alternative approach should be put in place and the rationale recorded. Line managers should be kept informed about the process in train.

Keeping an accurate record of every step in this process is crucial—the facts of the complaint, the first meeting, the action agreed and signed records of the final meeting. Such records are important proof that the issue has been taken seriously by the organisation, has been dealt with appropriately and that there was an attempt at resolution. It also provides evidence that the organisation has acted fairly to both sides in the process. Confidentiality is essential and breaches should be met with sanctions set out in advance.

Where the complaint has been deemed vexatious, the matter should be treated as a disciplinary issue.

Formal Process

If the issue cannot be resolved through an informal process, then a formal process should be instigated. This process will include a formal complaint and a formal investigation.

The Complaint Stage: in the formal process the complainant makes a formal complaint, usually in written form, setting out the alleged incidents, the dates on which they occurred and names of witnesses, where possible. This is signed and dated by the complainant. S/he should be assured by the organisation of its support during the course of this process.

The person complained of should receive a written notification that an allegation of bullying has been made against him/her. S/he should be assured of the organisation's presumption of innocence and of its support during the course of the process. Subsequent to this s/he should be given a copy of the complaint in full and any relevant documents, including a copy of the Bullying Prevention Policy. Both parties should be advised of the aims and objectives of the process, the procedures involved, the timeframe and the possible outcomes.

The Investigation Stage: terms of reference should set out the likely timeframe and scope of the investigation. The investigation should be carried out by a designated member of management or, where there is a possible conflict of interest, by an agreed external third party. As the Code states, the investigation *'should be conducted thoroughly, objectively, with sensitivity, utmost confidentiality, and with due respect for the rights of both the complainant and the person complained of.'*

The person investigating the complaint should meet with the complainant, with the person complained of and with any witnesses and relevant persons on an individual and confidential basis. The two parties at the core of the investigation should be afforded representation, usually by trade union/employee representative or a work colleague.

The investigation should be completed as quickly as possible. On completion, the investigator should provide the employer with a report, including his/her conclusions on the matter. The employer should provide the complainant and the person complained of with a copy of the report at the earliest opportunity and set a deadline within which a response can be made. On the basis of the report and any comments/responses made, the employer should decide on what action, if any, is to be taken. Both parties should be informed in writing of the next steps that will be taken.

Where the complaint is upheld, action should be taken to eliminate the risk of the behaviour continuing. The matter is now also a disciplinary issue and appropriate disciplinary procedures should be followed.

Where the complaint is not upheld the employer has a duty to the person complained against. Communicating the findings to both parties is essential, and also to anyone else who may have had prior knowledge of the complaint. Where the complaint has been made in good faith and not upheld, considerable sensitivity in the handling of the outcome is required. If the complaint is found to have been without basis and made maliciously, the employer's disciplinary procedures should be followed.

Appeals: an appeals mechanism should be available to both parties and appeals should be heard by a person of at least the same level of seniority as the original investigator, or more senior. For small organisations this may mean going outside the organisation.

Where internal procedures, formal or informal, fail to resolve a complaint of bullying, recourse may be had to the services of a Rights Commissioner at the LRC. Failure to deal adequately with allegations of bullying may result in legal action being taken through the courts. The High Court case of *Allen v Independent Newspapers* [2004] is an example of such an eventuality. Substantial damages were awarded to the plaintiff for personal injuries, loss and inconvenience caused by the alleged negligence of her former employer.

Vicarious Liability: an employer may be vicariously liable for the acts of bullying, harassment or sexual harassment against an employee carried out by a fellow employee or others s/he may deal with in the course of daily business.

In *Lister & Others v Hesley Hall Ltd* [2001] ALL R.R. 767 the English House of Lords held the defendant school liable for the acts of an employee who sexually assaulted pupils in his care. Lord Clyde stated as follows:

> It appears that the care and safekeeping of the boys had been entrusted to the respondents and they in turn had entrusted their care and safekeeping so far as the running of the boarding school was concerned to the warden … That function was one which the respondents had delegated to him. That he performed that function in a way which was an abuse of his position and abnegation of his duty does not sever the connection with his employment. The particular acts which he carried out upon the boys have been viewed not in isolation but in the context and the circumstances in which they occurred. Given that he had a general authority in the management of the house and in the care and supervision of the boys in it, the employers should be liable for the way in which he behaved towards them in his capacity as warden of the house. The respondents should then be vicariously liable to the appellants for the injury and damage which they suffered at the hands of the warden.

An important Irish case was *Shanley v Sligo County Council* [2001], which concerned a fireman who had been subjected to persistent bullying by a superior over a period of eight years. There was a catalogue of incidents, ranging from goading, spreading rumours and excessive criticism to using obscenities, threatening behaviour and aggression. An investigation had been undertaken by an independent body and its finding was that there was excessive bullying. It was also found that senior management were aware of the situation, but had not intervened. The plaintiff had suffered serious injury to his health as a result of the bullying. The Council admitted liability and was ordered to pay substantial costs to the plaintiff.

• Harassment

Harassment and sexual harassment are defined in law. Section 8 of the Equality Act 2004, amending s 14 of the Employment Equality Act 1998, provides that:

> —(1) For the purposes of this Act, where—
> (a) an employee (in this section referred to as 'the victim') is harassed or sexually harassed either at a place where the employee is employed (in this section referred to as 'the workplace') or otherwise in the course of his or her employment by a person who is—
>> (i) employed at that place or by the same employer,
>> (ii) the victim's employer, or
>> (iii) a client, customer or other business contact of the victim's employer and the circumstances of the harassment are such that the employer ought reasonably to have taken steps to prevent it,
> or
> (b) without prejudice to the generality of paragraph (a)—
>> (i) such harassment has occurred, and
>> (ii) either—
>>> (I) the victim is treated differently in the workplace or otherwise in the course of his or her employment by reason of rejecting or accepting the harassment, or
>>> (II) it could reasonably be anticipated that he or she would be so treated,
> the harassment or sexual harassment constitutes discrimination by the victim's employer in relation to the victim's conditions of employment.

Section 8(7): defines *harassment* in line with the Equality Directives and provides that:

> (i) references to harassment are to any form of unwanted conduct related to any of the discriminatory grounds, and

(ii) references to sexual harassment are to any form of unwanted verbal, non-verbal or physical conduct of a sexual nature,
being conduct which in either case has the purpose or effect of violating a person's dignity and creating an intimidating, hostile, degrading, humiliating or offensive environment for the person.
(b) Without prejudice to the generality of paragraph (a), such unwanted conduct may consist of acts, requests, spoken words, gestures or the production, display or circulation of written words, pictures or other material.

The conduct must be unwelcome and must be regarded as offensive, degrading or intimidating. The test is a subjective one, in that it is the victim who decides what is unwanted and whether or not it violates his/her dignity.

The *Code of Practice on Sexual Harassment and Harassment at Work 2002,* produced by the Equality Authority, categorises sexual harassment as:
* physical conduct of a sexual nature, e.g. unwanted conduct such as unnecessary touching, patting, pinching, assault;
* verbal conduct of a sexual nature, e.g. propositions, unwanted or offensive flirtations, suggestive remarks, lewd comments;
* non-verbal conduct of a sexual nature, e.g. displaying pornographic pictures, emails, text messages, leering, sexually suggestive gestures;
* sex-based conduct, e.g. derogatory or degrading abuse or insults that are gender-based.

Harassment concerns similar behaviour, but without the sexual element.

Workplace has a broad definition and may extend to a place of work-related socialising, including, for example, the office party, business functions, conferences, or social events where employees meet. (See the *Maguire* case in Chapter 8.)

Section 15: provides that the employer will be liable for any harassment of its employees. An employer may avail of the defence that such steps were taken as were reasonably practicable to prevent the employee's harassment. In this instance, the first line of defence would be to have a clear policy in place.

An Equality Tribunal case worth noting in this regard is *Ms Z v A Hotel* DEC–E2007-014. The case concerned the alleged sexual harassment of an employee and discriminatory treatment in that she was not re-engaged by the respondent after a period of lay-off.
Facts: the complainant commenced work as a casual part-time waitress with the respondent in October 2004. On the night of 7 December she attended the respondent's Christmas party in the company of a friend and work colleague, Ms

X. The complainant alleged that around 3.00am Mr A, the General Manager of the hotel, who was sitting alone at the time, beckoned her to sit beside him. He proceeded to tell her that she looked gorgeous that evening, that he wanted tô go home with her and that they should get a taxi together. She contended that he repeated this a number of times, although he did not touch her in an inappropriate manner. She submitted that this behaviour constituted sexual harassment of her contrary to the Employment Equality Acts 1998 and 2004. The complainant's version of events was roundly rejected by the respondent, who submitted that the complainant's behaviour had been inappropriate in that she had made advances on him.

In *Atkinson v Carthy and Others* [2005] ELR 1 an employee had been subjected to sexual harassment by the employer's accountant over a long period of time. She did not make a formal complaint and argued that there was no complaints procedure in place to allow her to make such a complaint. The employer argued that he had an open-door policy regarding employee complaints.

The Circuit Court held that:

> The failure of the defendants to have in place adequate procedures renders them liable and by reason of their failure to fulfill their statutory obligations they are responsible and cannot plead immunity from same simply because the plaintiff failed to make a complaint.

• Stress

In terms of labour law stress is a relatively recent phenomenon, but it is an area that has witnessed a significant increase in the amount of litigation it has attracted in recent years. In terms of the workplace, stress may result from harassment, bullying, victimisation, injury, pressure of work or overwork. The EU Framework Agreement on Work-Related Stress 2004 describes *stress* as being:

> … a state, which is accompanied by physical, psychological or social complaints or dysfunctions which results from individuals feeling unable to bridge a gap with the requirements or expectations placed on them.

Cases where stress has featured have been taken under health and safety legislation, as well as under common law principles.

An important Irish case in this area is *Berber v Dunnes Stores Ltd* [2006] HC. Here, the plaintiff commenced working with the defendant as a trainee manager in 1980 and until 1988 was employed as a store manager in various locations. In 1988 he moved to buying, where he remained until 2000, gradually moving up the ladder to men's 'ready-mades' buyer. During 2000 the situation changed considerably in that, unlike previous years, where as many as fifty days were spent abroad sourcing and buying merchandise, only one trip was taken, to a clothing show in Germany. There also appeared to be a new interest in his health, which was given as a reason for not sending him on a buying trip to the Far East. The plaintiff had suffered from Crohn's disease since his late teens and he was also colour-blind. In August the plaintiff was requested to report to the human resources department on his medical condition. In late 2000 he was requested by management to move from buying back to store management, which he viewed as a demotion. Based on assurances from the managing director that he would be fast-tracked to store manager or regional manager within six to twelve months, he agreed to return to store management, starting in the flagship Blanchardstown store, in ladies' wear. On arrival at the defendant's head office on 27 November, he discovered that he was being directed to homewares. He did not go to Blanchardstown. After three meetings with the director of stores' operations he was suspended from work, with pay.

In a review with his medical consultant on 13 December it was recorded that the plaintiff had been through an excessive amount of stress with his job and that this had not contributed to his well-being. He was certified as being unfit for work until 28 December. The plaintiff reported for work on 28 December, but only worked for four days before ceasing to work because of ill health. In relation to the subsequent exchange of solicitors' correspondence, the fact that the defendant sent responses directly to the plaintiff's house rather than to his solicitor served, Laffoy J. noted, to '*heighten the distrust of the plaintiff and increased the stress he was under*'.

Laffoy J. also stated that '*while some of his behaviour might be characterized as unreasonable it was attributable to the fact that his trust in the defendant's senior management and executives had been shattered*'.

The contention between the parties continued after the plaintiff returned to work in the Blanchardstown store at the end of April. The plaintiff's final day at work with the defendant was 15 May 2001, during which a heated argument developed that resulted in an alleged abusive verbal attack on the plaintiff within the hearing of other management staff.

In a letter to the managing director, dated 30 May, the plaintiff stated that he had been advised that the conduct of the defendant towards him amounted to a repudiation by the defendant of its obligations to him and that his contract of employment had therefore come to an end. He also referred to the fact that his consultant had advised him that in the interests of his health, he must cease working in the environment immediately.

The plaintiff's claim fell under two main headings:

1. For breach of contract in that he was constructively and wrongfully dismissed.
2. For personal injuries formulated both in contract and in tort.

On the plaintiff's submission that there was a series of breaches of contract amounting to repudiation, Laffoy J. did not agree:

> The correct interpretation of what happened is that the manner in which the defendant dealt with the plaintiff in the knowledge of the precarious nature of his physical and psychological health viewed objectively amounted to oppressive conduct. It was likely to seriously damage their employer/employee relationship and it did so. Accordingly, the defendant breached its obligation to maintain the plaintiff's trust and confidence ... A breach by an employer of its implied obligation to maintain trust and confidence of an employee is a breach which goes to the root of the contract.

It was decided that the defendant had indeed unlawfully repudiated the contract of employment.

On the personal injuries claim, Laffoy J. did not consider it necessary to distinguish between the two causes of action in contract and in tort and made reference to the English High Court case of *Walker v Northumberland* [1995] 1 ALL E.R. 737 at 759, where Colman J. had pointed out that:

> the scope of the duty of care owed to an employee to take reasonable care to provide a safe system of work is co-extensive with the implied term as to the employee's safety in the contract of employment.

This statement was later approved by the Court of Appeal in *Gogay v Hertfordshire County Council* [2000] IRLR 703.

On the question of liability, Laffoy J. held that the questions identified by Clarke J. in *Maher v Jabil Global Services Limited* [2005] 16 ELR 233 constituted the relevant questions and the proper approach:

> (a) has the plaintiff suffered an injury to his or her health as opposed to what might be described as ordinary occupational stress?
> (b) if so, is that injury attributable to the workplace? and
> (c) if so, was the harm suffered to the particular employee concerned reasonably foreseeable in all the circumstances?

In the end, the plaintiff was awarded €72,622: €40,000 in general damages and €32,622 in special damages/damages for breach of contract. The case is under appeal to the Supreme Court.

In the UK one of the most important cases in the area of work-related stress was the *Hatton* case. *Sutherland v Hatton* [2002] 2 ALL ER 1 concerned four conjoined appeals in which the employer was appealing against the finding of liability for the employee's psychiatric injury. Two of the plaintiffs were teachers in a comprehensive school, the third person was an administrative assistant at a local authority training centre, and the fourth person was a raw material operative in a factory. In this case Hale L.J. set down the tests to be applied in determining an employer's liability for stress-related psychiatric injury. The so-called *practical propositions* were identified as follows:

> (1) There are no special control mechanisms applying to claims for psychiatric (or physical) illness or injury arising from the stress of doing the work the employee is required to do. The ordinary principles of employer's liability apply.
>
> (2) The threshold question is whether this kind of harm to this particular employee was reasonably foreseeable: this has two components (a) an injury to health (as distinct from occupational stress) which (b) is attributable to stress at work (as distinct from other factors).
>
> (3) Foreseeability depends upon what the employer knows (or ought reasonably to know) about the individual employee. Because of the nature of mental disorder, it is harder to foresee than physical injury, but may be easier to foresee in a known individual than in the population at large. An employer is usually entitled to assume that the employee can withstand the normal pressures of the job unless he knows of some particular problem or vulnerability.
>
> (4) The test is the same whatever the employment: there are no occupations which should be regarded as intrinsically dangerous to mental health.
>
> (5) Factors likely to be relevant in answering the threshold question include:
>> (a) The nature and extent of the work done by the employee. Is the workload much more than is normal for the particular job? Is the work particularly intellectually or emotionally demanding for this employee? Are demands being made of this employee unreasonable when compared with the demands made of others in the same or comparable jobs? Or are there signs that others doing this job are suffering harmful

levels of stress? Is there an abnormal level of sickness or absenteeism in the same job or the same department?

(b) Signs from the employee of impending harm to health. Has he a particular problem or vulnerability? Has he already suffered from illness attributable to stress at work? Have there recently been frequent or prolonged absences which are uncharacteristic of him? Is there reason to think that these are attributable to stress at work, for example because of complaints or warnings from him or others?

(6) The employer is generally entitled to take what he is told by his employee at face value, unless he has good reason to think to the contrary. He does not generally have to make searching enquiries of the employee or seek permission to make further enquiries of his medical advisers.

(7) To trigger a duty to take steps, the indications of impending harm to health arising from stress at work must be plain enough for any reasonable employer to realise that he should do something about it.

(8) The employer is only in breach of duty if he has failed to take the steps which are reasonable in the circumstances, bearing in mind the magnitude of the risk of harm occurring, the gravity of the harm which may occur, the costs and practicability of preventing it, and the justifications for running the risk.

(9) The size and scope of the employer's operation, its resources and the demands it faces are relevant in deciding what is reasonable; these include the interests of other employees and the need to treat them fairly, for example, in any redistribution of duties.

(10) An employer can only reasonably be expected to take steps which are likely to do some good: the court is likely to need expert evidence on this.

(11) An employer who offers a confidential advice service, with referral to appropriate counselling or treatment services, is unlikely to be found in breach of duty.

(12) If the only reasonable and effective step would have been to dismiss or demote the employee, the employer will not be in breach of duty in allowing a willing employee to continue in the job.

(13) In all cases, therefore, it is necessary to identify the steps which the employer both could and should have taken before finding him in breach of his duty of care.

(14) The claimant must show that that breach of duty has caused or materially contributed to the harm suffered. It is not enough

to show that occupational stress has caused the harm.

(15) Where the harm suffered has more than one cause, the employer should only pay for that proportion of the harm suffered which is attributable to his wrongdoing, unless the harm is truly indivisible. It is for the defendant to raise the question of apportionment.

(16) The assessment of damages will take account of any pre-existing disorder or vulnerability and of the chance that the claimant would have succumbed to a stress-related disorder in any event.

chapter 6

LEVE

> This chapter will consider the employee's entitlement to leave from
> the workplace, including:
> - holiday leave;
> - public holidays;
> - leave in respect of maternity;
> - parental leave;
> - *force majeure*;
> - carer's leave;
> - adoptive leave;
> - sick leave;
> - leave to facilitate jury service.

• Leave

An employee's entitlement to leave from work is based either in statute or in the
employee's contract of employment.

Statutory rights to leave are found in the following Acts:
- Organisation of Working Time Act 1997—annual leave and public holidays;
- Adoptive Leave Act 1995–2005—adoptive leave;
- Carer's Leave Act 2001 as amended—carer's leave;
- Maternity Protection Acts 1994–2004—maternity leave;
- Parental Leave Acts 1998–2006—parental leave and *force majeure* leave.

Other leave entitlements will depend on the individual contracts of employment,
but may include sick leave, compassionate leave, career-break leave, study and
exam leave and jury service leave.

Sick Leave

There is no statutory entitlement to sick leave. The right of an employee to avail
of sick leave, be it paid or unpaid, is purely a contractual matter and will be
determined by what is contained in the employee's contract of employment in
that regard. Section 3(1)(k) of the Terms of Employment (Information) Act 1994
obliges an employer to provide particulars in writing of any terms or conditions
relating to incapacity for work due to sickness or injury and paid sick leave.

Certain employment sectors covered by Employment Regulation Orders or
Registered Employment Agreements have binding arrangements in respect of sick

leave. These sectors include Contract Cleaning, Construction, Electrical Contractors, Drapery & Footwear in the Dublin area, Hairdressing (Dublin, Bray) and Law Clerks.

Organisation of Working Time Act 1997

Recent research findings from EuroFound (the European Foundation for the Improvement of Living and Working Conditions) show that Ireland ranks lowest in the former EU 15 for the number of days' leave entitlement, with twenty-nine days of combined annual and public holiday leave. Workers in Sweden have the highest number with forty-two days' leave (combining annual leave and public holidays). The EU 15 have 35.6 days of combined leave, while workers in the twelve new Member States have on average 31.3 days, giving the EU 27 an average of 33.7 days. After Sweden, the countries with the greatest number of days' leave are Germany (forty days), Italy (thirty-nine days) and Luxembourg and Denmark (thirty-eight days each). The countries with the lowest number of days' leave are Hungary (twenty-eight days), Latvia (twenty-seven days) and Estonia (twenty-six days).

Annual Leave

Section 19 of the Organisation of Working Time Act 1997 provides that employees are entitled to the following paid annual leave (whichever is the greater):
- four working weeks in a leave year in which the employee works at least 1,365 hours;
- one-third of a working week for each month in the leave year for which s/he works at least 117 hours;
- 8 per cent of the hours the employee works in a leave year (subject to a maximum of four working weeks).

Public Holidays

There are nine annual public holidays, namely:
- New Year's Day (1 January);
- St Patrick's Day (17 March);
- Easter Monday;
- first Monday in May;
- first Monday in June;
- first Monday in August;
- last Monday in October;
- Christmas Day (25 December);
- St Stephen's Day (26 December).

Other provisions of the Act include:
Section 11, which sets out minimum rest periods of not less than eleven hours in any twenty-four-hour period.

Section 12, which provides that an employer shall not require an employee to work for a period of more than four hours and thirty minutes without allowing a break of at least fifteen minutes.

Section 15, which places limits on the weekly working hours. An employee may not work for more than an average of forty-eight hours per week, calculated over a reference period.

In *O'Malley v Liachavicius* DWT074 2007 the issues of excessive working hours, inadequate rest periods, failure to provide annual and public holidays and failure to keep records came up for consideration before the Labour Court. The case was brought by way of an appeal by the claimant of a decision of a Rights Commissioner on the grounds that the compensation awarded to him was too low in the circumstances.

Facts: the claimant was employed as a plasterer by the respondent company from September 2005 to February 2006. He argued that he had worked excessive hours and was not granted adequate daily rest periods. When he was required to work up to seven days a week on occasion, he was not given appropriate rest periods. He was not paid adequately for annual leave and his employer had failed to keep records of his working time, as required under the Act. The company disputed these arguments, stating that the employee worked a forty-hour, five-day week, that he was not a plasterer but rather a general operative in receipt of pay rates exceeding those prescribed for the industry, that he had received holiday pay and that the records were incomplete for that period owing to the illness of the company's accountant.

The Court accepted that the claimant had worked as a general operative. The respondent had failed in his obligation to maintain records and as such he had to bear the burden of rebutting the claimant's evidence. The Court held that he had not rebutted the evidence to its satisfaction. The Court referred to an earlier decision of the Labour Court:

> In *Cementation Skanska (Formerly Kavaerner Cementation) v Carroll* Labour Court Determination WTC0338 (October 28, 2003) this Court stated as follows in relation to the computation of compensation for failure to provide annual leave in accordance with the Act:

> 'The obligation to provide annual leave is imposed for health and safety reasons and the right to leave has been characterized as a fundamental social right in European law (see comments of Advocate General Tizzano in *R v Secretary of State for Trade and Industry, ex parte Broadcasting, Entertainment, Cinematography and Theatre Union* [2001] IRLR 559 which were quoted with

approval by Lavin J. in the *Royal Liver* case. In *Von Colson and Kaman v Land Nordrhein–Westfalen* [1984] E.C.R. 1891 the ECJ has made it clear that where such a right is infringed the judicial redress provided should not only compensate for economic loss sustained but must provide a real deterrent against future infractions.'

The Court was of the view that similar consideration should apply in the instant case:

> The Claimant was deprived of holiday pay to which he was entitled by law. He was also required to work excessive hours without adequate breaks and so imperil his health and safety at work. The Claimant is a native of a foreign country and was unfamiliar with his rights in Irish law and practice. The Respondent failed to respond to requests from the Claimant (made on advice of his solicitor) for information concerning his terms of employment. He was not given a P60 or his P45 at the time these documents should have been furnished. Finally the Respondent failed to attend before the Rights Commissioner to answer the Claimant's complaints. While certain explanations were offered for these omissions, the Court does not consider that any of them provide an adequate excuse.

The Court allowed the appeal and increased the earlier award from €2,500 to €5,000.

Section 20: provides that the employer shall determine the times at which annual leave is granted to an employee. In this regard the employer must take certain issues into account, i.e. the employee's family/work balance and employee consultation.

This issue arose in the Labour Court case of *An Post v Christopher Burke* (WTC/05/61 Determination No.066). On 13 December 2004 the claimant had put in a request for annual leave for the first two weeks of January 2005. An Post refused the request and a subsequent request made on 21 December, stating that a period of extended leave was not possible owing to industrial relations problems in the area. On the question of entitlement to two weeks' unbroken leave, a Rights Commissioner found that his right to two weeks' unbroken leave had not been infringed as he had taken two weeks' leave in May. On appeal to the Labour Court and on the question of whether the employer can determine when leave is taken, the Court determined that:

> the employer does have the entitlement to determine the period

of annual leave and by inference is entitled to decide that an operational reason is a reasonable ground for refusing annual leave provided that the employer has met with the other requirements of the Act.

Failure to keep records
Section 25: obliges an employer to keep records showing compliance in respect of employees.

Absences
There is no general obligation on an employer to pay an employee who is absent during the course of work.

Sick leave
Rights to pay in respect of absences are to be found in employment agreements, contracts or recognised custom and practice. There is no statutory entitlement to be paid while on sick leave.

Parental Leave Act 1998 and Parental Leave (Amendment Act) 2006
Implementing EU Directive 96/34/EC, this Act came into operation on 3 December 1998 and confers an entitlement to parental leave and *force majeure* leave on qualifying employees. It stipulates certain qualifying conditions that must be satisfied in order for an employee to avail of the entitlements.

The Acts provide that an employee who is the natural or adoptive parent of a child or who is acting *in loco parentis* to a child is entitled to:
* leave for a period of fourteen weeks to take care of that child;
* which leave must be taken before the child reaches the age of eight years or in the case of a child with a disability sixteen years;
* in the case of an adopted child who has, on or before the date of the adoption order, reached the age of six years but is under eight years of age, leave may be taken not later than two years from the date of the adoption order.

The leave may be taken as a block of continuous leave of fourteen weeks or, with the agreement of the employer, as separate periods each consisting of not less than six weeks or by reduced working hours.

In the case of a disabled child, s 2 defines *disability* as:

> ... an enduring physical, sensory, mental health or intellectual impairment of the child such that the level of care required for the child is substantially more than the level of care that is generally required for children of the same age who do not have any such impairment.

Generally, in order to be entitled to take the leave an employee must have completed one year's continuous service with the employer. However, where an employee does not have the required continuous service but has completed three months on the latest day for commencing the leave, s/he will be entitled to *pro rata* parental leave. In such a case the employee will be entitled to one week's leave for every month of continuous employment completed with the employer when the leave begins.

An employee is entitled to parental leave in respect of each child of whom s/he is the parent. This leave may not exceed fourteen weeks in any twelve-month period without the consent of the employer.

When an employee proposes to take parental leave, s/he must, as soon as is reasonably practicable, but not later than six weeks before the leave begins, give written notice of the proposal to the employer, setting out details of commencement date, duration of leave and the manner in which it is to be taken. These subsequently form part of a confirmation document that is signed by both the employee and employer.

The employer may require an employee to provide evidence of his/her entitlement to parental leave (e.g. child's date of birth, date of adoption order or nature of the child's disability). The leave must be for the care of a child. Where an employer has reasonable grounds for believing that the leave is not being used for the purpose of taking care of the child concerned, s/he may terminate the leave. The employee must be given seven days' notice in writing of the intention to terminate the leave. The employee has the right to make submissions in such cases, which must be considered by the employer before deciding whether to terminate the leave.

An employer may postpone the parental leave if s/he is satisfied that granting the leave would have a substantial adverse effect on the operation of his/her business. The postponement may be for a period not exceeding six months, to a date agreed by both the employer and the employee. Generally only one postponement is allowed under the Act, unless there are seasonal variations in the volume of work.

Unpaid leave
Section 15: provides that an employee is entitled to return to work at the end of the period of parental leave, to the job held immediately prior to the leave and under the same contract, terms and conditions of employment, incorporating any improvements to such conditions.

Section 16: provides that if it is not reasonably practicable for an employer or his/her successor to allow the employee to return under these conditions, the employer must offer the employee suitable alternative employment.

Force Majeure Leave

Section 13(1) of the Parental Leave Act 1998, as amended by the 2006 Act, provides that:

> An employee shall be entitled to leave with pay from his or her employment, to be known ... as force majeure leave where, for urgent family reasons, owing to an injury to or the illness of a person specified in subsection (2), the immediate presence of the employee at the place where the person is, whether at his or her home or elsewhere, is indispensable.

The persons referred to in subsection (2), as amended by s 8 of the 2006 Act, are:
- the employee's child;
- the co-habiting spouse or partner;
- brother, sister, parent, grandparent;
- a person to whom the employee is *in loco parentis*;
- a person who resides with the employee in a relationship of domestic dependency.

Section 8: defines domestic dependency as occurring where, in the event of injury or illness, one reasonably relies on the other to make arrangements for the provision of care. The sexual orientation of the persons concerned is immaterial.

By its nature *force majeure* leave is unplanned as it is taken in situations of urgency. It is not leave one applies for in advance of the need arising. If, therefore, an employee has sufficient notice of a need to take leave, alternative arrangements, such as holiday leave, should be taken.

When an employee takes *force majeure* leave s/he must inform the employer as soon as is reasonably practicable, detailing the dates on which the leave was taken and giving a statement of the facts as to the reasons it was taken. The information must be set out in the form prescribed under the Parental Leave (Notice of Force Majeure Leave) Regulations 1998 S.I. 454/1998, known as the *scheduled form,* or a form to like effect.

Force majeure leave may consist of one or more days, but may not exceed three days in any period of twelve consecutive months or five days in thirty-six consecutive months.

Where an employee is on leave for part of a day only, it is deemed to be a full day. *Force majeure* leave is paid leave. It cannot be treated as part of any other leave, e.g. sick leave, maternity leave, annual leave or parental leave.

In *Carey v Penn Racquet Sports Ltd* [2001] the High Court, on appeal from the

EAT, considered what constituted *urgent, immediate and indispensable* for the purposes of *force majeure* leave. The facts as set before the EAT were as follows: an employee who was a single mother of an eight-year-old child did not come to work on 11 June 1999 because her child was ill. The child had been ill in the early hours (between midnight and 6.00am) and when the mother got up for work commencing at 8.00am, she noticed the child had a rash on her legs. She decided to stay at home to observe her. The rash was getting worse and she took her to the doctor, 3 miles away. She was advised by the doctor to get calamine lotion, which she bought from a pharmacy 10 miles away. She felt it was best to stay with her child, to monitor her progress. She lived alone about 20 miles from her workplace and had a childminder. The company refused to grant her *force majeure* leave.

The EAT upheld the company's decision by a majority, determining that '*the particulars of the case did not fall within the meaning of the Act, as urgent, immediate and indispensable*'.

On appeal from that decision the matter came before the High Court in 2001. Carroll J. stated that:

> While it is not spelt out in the determination of the Tribunal it seems clear that the reason the force majeure leave was refused was that the rash turned out to be not serious. In my opinion the Tribunal should not have approached the matter on that basis. This was judging with hindsight the urgency of the family reasons and the question of whether the employee's presence with her child was indispensable. The matter should have been looked at from the plaintiff's point of view at the time the decision was made not to go to work. Also the plaintiff could not be assumed to have medical knowledge which she did not possess.

Carroll J. decided that it was a mistake in law to decide on the basis of the ultimate outcome of the illness in the case. The plaintiff was awarded one day of paid *force majeure* leave and was also deemed entitled to her costs.

This decision was upheld in the subsequent case of *McGaley v Liebherr Container Crane* [2001] 3 IR 563, where McCracken J. affirmed Carroll J.'s decision:

> This is clear authority that the Tribunal must judge whether the facts of the particular case come within Section 13 but that such judgement must be based on the facts as they existed at the time of the circumstances which it is alleged gave rise to the implementation of the Section.

In *Foley v Dunnes Stores* [2005] the employee's husband fell ill suddenly with appendicitis. The employee was paid for *force majeure* leave for that day. The employee informed her employer that she also intended taking *force majeure* leave on the day her husband would be discharged from hospital. It was held that she had failed to show that her immediate presence was indispensable on the day in question.

An employer is obliged under the Acts to keep records of any parental leave and *force majeure* leave taken by employees. Details of periods of employment of each employee and the dates and times of the leave taken must be outlined. These records must be retained for a period of eight years.

Carer's Leave

The Carer's Leave Act 2001, as amended by the Social Welfare Law Reform and Pensions Act 2006 (amended by the Social Welfare and Pensions Act 2007), confers the right on qualifying employees to take unpaid leave from their employment for up to 104 weeks to look after relevant persons in need of full-time care and attention.

Section 6: stipulates that in order to qualify for the leave entitlement, the employee must have been employed for a period of twelve months' continuous employment with the employer from whose employment the carer's leave is proposed to be taken.

The employee must provide full-time care and attention for a *relevant person*, who is defined under the Social Welfare (Consolidation) Act 1993, as amended by the Social Welfare Act 2000, as a person who has such a disability that s/he requires full-time care and attention, being such person who:
- has reached the age of eighteen; or
- if under eighteen years, is a person in respect of whom an allowance is paid for domiciliary care of handicapped children.

A relevant person will be regarded as requiring full-time care and attention where s/he has such a disability that s/he requires from another person:
- continual supervision and frequent assistance throughout the day in connection with normal bodily functions, e.g. eating, dressing, mobility;
- continual supervision in order to avoid danger to him/herself; and
- the nature and extent of the disability has been certified in the prescribed manner by a medical practitioner.

Section 6(5): provides that an employee who proposes taking carer's leave must acquire a decision from a deciding officer of the Department of Social, Community and Family Affairs that the person in respect of whom the leave is to be taken is a relevant person for the purposes of the Act. A copy of this decision must be given to the employer as soon as the employee receives it.

Originally carer's leave was for a period of sixty-five weeks, but that was increased to 104 weeks in the 2006 Act.

While providing full-time care the carer is permitted to attend a course of education or training or voluntary or community work or to engage in limited self-employment in his/her home or to engage in employment outside the home provided that the time spent at this activity does not exceed fifteen hours per week. This activity must be approved by the Minister for Social, Community and Family Affairs.

Carer's leave may be taken in the form of:
• a continuous period of 104 weeks;
• a number of periods, the aggregate duration of which does not exceed a total of 104 weeks.

Section 13: provides that an employee on carer's leave will be regarded as still working for all purposes relating to his/her employment and none of his/her rights shall be affected, with the exception of rights to remuneration, certain annual and public holiday leave, superannuation benefits and obligations to pay employment contributions.

Section 14: provides that upon termination of the leave period, the employee is entitled to return to work:

> (a) with the employer with whom he or she was working immediately before the start of the period or, where during the employee's absence from work there was or were a change or changes of ownership of the undertaking in which the employee was employed immediately before the absence, the owner on the expiration of the period (the successor),
> (b) the job that the employee held immediately before the commencement of the period, and
> (c) under the contract of employment in respect of which the employee was employed immediately before the commencement of the period or, where a change of ownership such as is referred to in paragraph (a) has occurred, under a contract of employment with the successor, that is identical to the contract under which the employee was employed immediately before such commencement, and (in either case) under terms or conditions not less favourable to the employee than those that would have been applicable to him or her if he or she had not been so absent from work.

Section 15: allows that where it is not reasonably practicable for the employer to allow the employee to return in accordance with s 14 above, the employee is entitled to be offered suitable alternative employment.

Adoptive Leave
The Adoptive Leave Acts 1995–2005 confer an entitlement to female employees and, in certain circumstances, to male employees to employment leave for the purpose of child adoption.

Section 2: defines *adopting parent* as an adopting mother, an adopting father or a sole male adopter. These categories are defined as follows:

- *Adopting mother* means a woman, including an employed adopting mother, in whose care a child (of whom she is not the natural mother) has been placed or is to be placed with a view to the making of an adoption order, or to the effecting of a foreign adoption or following any such adoption.
- *Sole male adopter* means a male employee who is not an adopting father within the meaning above and in whose sole care a child has been placed or is to be placed with a view to the making of an adoption order, or to the effecting of a foreign adoption or following any such adoption.
- *Adopting father* means a male employee in whose care a child has been placed or is to be placed with a view to the making of an adoption order, or to the effecting of a foreign adoption or following any such adoption, where the adopting mother has died.

Section 3 of the 2005 Act provides for minimum periods of leave for adopting mothers and sole male adopters and for other adopting fathers in certain, limited circumstances. The periods of leave currently stand at twenty-four consecutive weeks of adoptive leave and a period of additional adoptive leave of sixteen consecutive weeks' unpaid leave immediately following the twenty-four-week period.

Generally, there is no obligation on an employer to pay an employee while on adoptive leave, however the employee may be entitled to a social welfare payment. Such payment will attach to the twenty-four-week period of leave only and not to the additional leave period.

The employee is obliged under the Act to inform the employer at least four weeks before the expected date of placement of the intention to take adoptive leave and to provide a certificate of placement not later than four weeks after the day of placement or, in the case of a foreign adoption, particulars in writing of the placement as soon as is reasonably practicable.

Where an adopting mother dies, the adopting father is entitled to adoptive leave for:

- the standard twenty-four weeks; or
- where the adopting mother dies on or after the day of placement, twenty-four weeks less the period equivalent to the period beginning on the day of placement and ending on the day of her death; or
- such period as the Minister may prescribe.

Section 11A: provides for an entitlement to time off without loss of pay to attend pre-adoption classes or meetings that the employee is obliged to attend.

Section 15: provides for a general right to return to work after the adoptive leave or additional adoptive leave has expired:

> (a) either:
>> (i) with the employer with whom the employee was working immediately before the absence, or
>> (ii) if during the absence there was a change of ownership of the undertaking in which the employee was employed immediately before the absence, with the owner (the successor)
>
> (b) in the job which the employee held immediately before the absence began, and
>
> (c) under the contract of employment under which the employee was employed immediately before the absence began, or (as the case may be) under a contract of employment with the successor, which is identical to the contract under which the employee was employed immediately before the absence and (in either case) under terms and conditions
>> (i) that are not less favourable than those that would have been applicable, and
>> (ii) that incorporate any improvements in the terms and conditions of employment to which the employee would have been entitled if the employee had not been so absent from work.

Where returning to the job held immediately before the absence is not practicable, suitable alternative work must be provided.

Section 19: obliges the employee to inform the employer, in writing, of the employee's intention to return to work and of the date on which the employee expects to do so. Generally, this must be done at least four weeks before the expected date of return.

Maternity Leave
The Maternity Protection Act 1994, as amended by the 2004 Act, was introduced to give effect to Council Directive 92/85/EEC on measures to encourage

improvements in the safety, health and welfare at work of pregnant workers and workers who have recently given birth or who are breastfeeding. These Acts set down the minimum legal entitlements in respect of maternity issues at work. There is nothing preventing more generous entitlements from being provided or negotiated between employers and employees.

The Maternity Protection Acts 1994 and 2004 contain provisions in relation to:
- maternity leave;
- time off for ante-natal and post-natal care or classes;
- father's leave in the event of the death of the mother;
- time off from work or a reduction of working hours for breastfeeding;
- the right to return to work once leave expires;
- protection against dismissal.

In addition to the Maternity Protection Acts the Employment Equality Acts 1998–2004, the Safety, Health and Welfare at Work Act 2005 also provides protection in relation to pregnancy, maternity leave and other related matters.

The 1994 Act, as amended by the 2004 Act, sets out the entitlement to maternity leave. The entitlement is to:
- twenty-six consecutive weeks, which is to commence not later than two weeks before the last day of the expected week of confinement (s 8);
- additional unpaid leave of sixteen consecutive weeks to commence immediately on the expiry of the twenty-six weeks (s 14).

The twenty-six- and sixteen-week periods represent an increase from twenty-two weeks and twelve weeks respectively and are effective for women who commence maternity leave after 1 March 2007. When the Act was passed in 1994 the entitlement was to fourteen weeks' maternity leave, with a right to additional leave for a maximum period of four weeks.

In addition to the above periods of leave, there is also an entitlement to:
- time off from work without loss of pay for ante-natal or post-natal care;
- time off work to attend ante-natal classes without loss of pay. The father also has a once-off entitlement to attend the last two ante-natal classes without loss of pay;
- extension of the maternity leave where the date of confinement occurs in the week after the expected week of confinement (s 12);
- time off from work or a reduction of working hours for breastfeeding in accordance with regulations made by the Minister in this regard.

The most significant entitlement under the Acts is the right to maternity leave.

Section 9: places an obligation on the employee to provide notification in writing to the employer of her intention to take maternity leave. A medical certificate or other appropriate certificate confirming the pregnancy and specifying the expected week of confinement must also be provided. The employer should be informed as soon as is reasonably practicable, but not later than four weeks before the commencement of the maternity leave.

However, it would appear from case law that even where an employee has failed to notify the employer, she may still be entitled to maternity entitlements under the Acts. Section 14A concerns terminating the period of additional maternity leave in the event of sickness of the mother, where this occurs during the last four weeks of maternity leave or during the period of additional maternity leave. In such circumstances the employee may request her employer, in writing, to terminate her period of additional leave. This entitlement is at the discretion of the employer.

The employee's absence from work due to sickness following such termination shall be treated in the same manner as any absence from work of the employee due to sickness.

Section 14B: concerns the postponement of maternity leave or additional maternity leave in the event of the hospitalisation of the child in respect of whom the maternity leave is taken. The employee may ask her employer, in writing, to postpone:
- part of the maternity leave;
- part of the maternity leave and the additional maternity leave; or
- the additional maternity leave or part of it.

Maternity leave may be postponed only where the employee has taken at least fourteen weeks' maternity leave and not less than four of those weeks were after the end of the week of confinement. This entitlement is at the discretion of the employer. Where the leave is granted, the employee is entitled to take the postponed maternity leave or additional maternity leave in one continuous block, known as *resumed leave*, commencing not later than seven days after the discharge of the child from hospital.

Section 15A: provides the entitlement to time off work without loss of pay to attend ante-natal classes. The provision is for attendance at one set of ante-natal classes (other than the last three classes in such a set) and those classes may be attended during one or more pregnancies. Provision is also made for the once-off entitlement for the expectant father to time off work, without loss of pay, for the purpose of attending the least two ante-natal classes in a set of such classes attended by the expectant mother before the birth of the child.

Section 15B: provides for the entitlement to time off work or a reduction of working hours without loss of pay for the purpose of breastfeeding. In this section *breastfeeding* includes expressing breast milk and feeding it to a child immediately or storing it for the purpose of feeding it to the child at a later time. Regulations under this section make provision for:

- the amount of time off and the number and frequency of breaks to which an employee is entitled;
- the reduction of working hours to which an employee is entitled;
- the terms and conditions relating to time off;
- the period of notice to be given to the employer.

An employer is not obliged to provide facilities for breastfeeding in the workplace if the provision of such facilities would give rise to a cost, other than a nominal cost, to the employer.

Section 16, as amended by s 10 of the 2004 Act: deals with the situation where the mother has delivered a living child but she dies before the expiry of the thirty-second week following the week of her confinement. In this instance, the father of the child will be entitled to take leave. The period of leave will be determined by when the mother's death occurred. Leave commences within seven days of the mother's death.

Health and Safety Leave
Sections 17–20: provide for leave on health and safety grounds. Employees to whom this applies include:

- pregnant employees;
- employees who have recently given birth; and
- employees who are breastfeeding.

In *Doorty v UCD* E2004-043 the issue of health and safety leave arose.

Facts: the complainant was a research scientist who claimed that she had been discriminated against on the ground of gender when she had been placed on health and safety leave during her pregnancy. A risk assessment had been carried out of her work and workplace, which found that chemicals being used in experiments carried out by the complainant posed a serious risk to her unborn child. The complainant expressed an interest in alternative work, such as lecturing. The respondent contended that no suitable alternative work was available and it had no choice but to put her on health and safety leave.

The Equality Officer found that the respondent had discriminated against the complainant on the ground of gender. It was noted that the complainant's pregnancy caused difficulties for the respondent in that it had obligations to an external body that funded the project in which the complainant was involved. However, the respondent also had obligations to the complainant for the duration of her contract of employment. The Equality Officer was not satisfied that adequate consideration had been given to alternatives to the health and safety leave.

The Safety, Health and Welfare at Work (General Applications) Regulations 2007 (Regulation 149) require an employer to:

> (a) assess any risk to the safety or health of employees and any possible effect on the pregnancy of, or breastfeeding by, employees resulting from any activity at that employer's place of work likely to involve a risk of exposure to any agent, process or working condition ... for that purpose determine the (i) nature, (ii) degree and (iii) duration of any employee's exposure to any agent, process or working condition
> (b) take preventive and protective measures to ensure the safety and health of such employees and avoid any possible effect on such pregnancy or breastfeeding.

Where the risk assessment carried out under Regulation 149 reveals a risk and where it is not practicable to ensure the safety and health of the employee through protective or preventive measures, the employer is obliged to adjust temporarily the working conditions or the working hours or both, and where that is not feasible to provide the employee with suitable alternative work.

Section 18 of the Maternity Protection Act provides that where it is not feasible to move the employee or where the alternative work is unsuitable, the employee will be granted leave known as *health and safety leave*. In these circumstances the employee is entitled to receive, on foot of a request to the employer, a certificate setting out the reasons why the leave was given, the date it commenced and its expected duration.

Other work is *suitable* if it is of a kind that is suitable to the employee concerned and appropriate for the employee to do in all the circumstances. Clearly the term *suitable* is to be taken subjectively, from the employee's viewpoint. Failure by an employer to provide suitable alternative work may entitle the employee to terminate the contract and thus bring a possible constructive dismissal claim under the Unfair Dismissal Act.

An employee who is granted health and safety leave is entitled to her usual remuneration for the first twenty-one days of her leave.

Regulation 151 of Safety, Health and Welfare at Work (General Application) Regulations 2007 provides that where an employee has a medical certificate stating that for health and safety reasons she should not be required to perform night work during pregnancy or for fourteen weeks following childbirth, the employer shall transfer her to daytime work or, where that is not technically or objectively feasible, shall grant her leave or extend the maternity leave. Night work is defined as taking place between the hours of 11.00pm and 6.00am, where the employee works at least three hours in that period as a normal course or where at least 25 per cent of the employee's monthly working time is performed during that period.

Section 22, as inserted by s 14 of the 2004 Act: provides that where an employee is on:

- maternity leave or additional maternity leave,
- father's leave (in the event of the mother's death) or additional father's leave,
- health and safety leave,
- time off for ante-natal care or classes or post-natal care,
- time off or reduced hours for breastfeeding,

then that employee is deemed to be in the employment of the employer while absent. A period of absence from work in these circumstances may not be treated as part of any other leave, including sick leave or annual leave.

Section 23, as amended by s 15 of the 2004 Act: provides that any purported termination of an employee's employment or suspension of that employment is void while the employee is absent from work owing to:

- maternity leave or additional maternity leave;
- father's leave or additional father's leave;
- health and safety leave;
- ante-natal or post-natal care or classes;
- breastfeeding.

A dismissal of an employee is automatically unfair if it results from the employee's pregnancy or related matters. Dismissals in such circumstances are taken under either the Unfair Dismissals Acts 1977–2007 (except where the employee falls into a category of excluded employees) or the Employment Equality Acts 1998–2004 on grounds of sex or marital status. Eligibility rules requiring fifty-two weeks' continuous service under the Unfair Dismissals Act do not apply in these circumstances.

An important case in this area was the Art 177 Reference to the ECJ by the House of Lords in *Brown v Rentokil Ltd* (1998) C-394/96. In this case the House of Lords asked if it was contrary to the Equal Treatment Directive to dismiss a female employee at any time during her pregnancy as a result of absence through illness arising from that pregnancy. The ECJ held that Arts 2(1) and 5(1) of Directive 76/207 precluded the dismissal of a female worker at any time during her pregnancy for absences due to incapacity for work caused by illness resulting from that pregnancy. The fact that the female worker was dismissed during her pregnancy on the basis of a contractual term providing that the employer may dismiss employees of either sex after a stipulated number of weeks of continuous absence did not have any bearing on the situation.

Section 26 of the Maternity Protection Act 1994, as amended by s 18 of the 2004 Act: provides that upon expiry of leave there is an entitlement to:

*   return to work with the same employer or the new owner (if there has been a change of owner);
*   return to the same job;
*   under the same contract; and
*   under terms and conditions that are not less favourable than those that would have applied had s/he not been absent; and
*   incorporate any improvements to the terms and conditions to which the employee would have been entitled if s/he had not been absent.

Section 27: provides that where it is not reasonably practicable for the employee to return to his/her old job, s/he is entitled to be offered suitable alternative employment by the employer, under a new contract. Suitable alternative work is work that is suitable and appropriate for the employee to do in the circumstances, under terms and conditions that are not less favourable than the original contract and which incorporate any improvements in those terms and conditions which the employee would have enjoyed had s/he not been absent.

In *Walsh v Tesco Ireland Ltd* DEE062 an employee alleged discrimination on grounds of her gender when her employer did not allow her to return to work on a part-time basis following maternity leave. In this case the complainant was employed as a general sales assistant with the respondent from November 1989. In December 1997 she went on maternity leave and returned to work in May 1998. Both before the maternity leave and upon her return the complainant requested to be placed on part-time hours. Owing to staff shortages over the summer holiday period, the respondent was not in a position to accede to her request. She was, however, allowed to have every Friday and every second Saturday off.

The Equality Officer found that the claimant had not been discriminated against. On appeal to the Labour Court, the Court determined that the respondent had acted reasonably in respect of the complainant having regard to the needs of the business. The complainant had failed to establish that she had been discriminated against on the ground of gender. Accordingly, the decision of the Equality Officer was upheld.

There is an obligation on the employee to the employer regarding notification of the intention to return to work.

In the landmark ruling of *McKenna v North Western Health Board* [2005] ECJ, the issue of sick leave during pregnancy was examined. The case concerned a claim by McKenna that her employer had discriminated against her on gender grounds, under the Employment Equality Act 1998, when the company offset pregnancy-related illness against the provisions of its sick leave scheme, resulting in a reduction to half pay.

The claimant, Ms McKenna, was employed by the Board as an assistant staff officer. She became pregnant in 2000 and was obliged to take sick leave as a result of a pregnancy-related illness that extended for almost the full duration of her pregnancy.

The Board's sick leave scheme provided for six months on full pay and six months on half pay in any period of four years. Full pay is received for a maximum of 183 days' incapacity in any period of twelve months, with any additional sick leave taken within the same twelve-month period attracting half pay only up to a maximum total of 365 days' leave within that four-year period. Employees were also entitled to receive full pay during the period of their maternity leave. The complainant was granted sick pay in accordance with the respondent's sick pay scheme. No distinction was made in the scheme between pregnancy-related illnesses and other forms of illness. Having taken 183 days of sick leave, Ms McKenna had exhausted her right to full pay and, accordingly, her pay was reduced to 50 per cent. She challenged the application of the sick leave scheme to her situation before the Equality Officer. Her contention was that by failing to differentiate between pregnancy-related illness and other illness, her employer had acted in a discriminatory manner. She also contended that putting her on half pay after the 183-day period constituted unfavourable treatment in respect of pay.

In her submission she cited the *Dekker* case (C-177/88), where the ECJ had held that unfavourable treatment because of pregnancy was direct discrimination on the ground of sex. In *Dekker* the issue concerned the refusal to appoint a woman on the ground of her pregnancy. She also referred to a number of Labour Court determinations, including *An Foras Forbartha v A Worker* DEE4/1982 and *Rathfarnham Inn v Kinsella* EE05/90, cases preceding *Dekker*, where it had been held that less favourable treatment on the ground of pregnancy constituted indirect discrimination.

Following a finding in her favour in 2001 by an Equality Officer, the North Western Health Board appealed the decision to the Labour Court and it in turn referred certain matters to the ECJ. In a Reference to the European Court of Justice in 2003 for a preliminary ruling on the interpretation of Community law made by the Irish Labour Court, the ECJ was asked:

> (i) Does a sick leave scheme which treats employees suffering

from pregnancy related illnesses and from pathological illness in an identical manner come within the scope of the equal treatment Directive 76/207.

(ii) If such a scheme is within the scope of 76/207, is it contrary to the Directive for an employer to offset a period of absence due to incapacity caused by a pregnancy related illness arising during pregnancy against an employee's total entitlement to benefit under an occupational sick leave scheme.

(iii) If such a scheme is within the scope of 76/207, is an employer obliged to have in place special arrangements to cover absence from work due to incapacity caused by a pregnancy related illness arising during pregnancy.

(iv) Does a sick leave scheme which treats employees suffering from pregnancy related illness and pathological illness come within the scope of Article 141 of the EC Treaty on equal pay and the equal pay Directive 75/117.

(v) If such a scheme is within the scope of Article 141 and Directive 75/117, is it contrary to that Article and Directive for an employer to reduce a woman's pay after an absence from work for a designated period due to incapacity caused by a pregnancy related illness arising during pregnancy in circumstances in which a non pregnant woman or man absent from work for the same period as a result of incapacity due to a pathological illness would suffer the same reduction.

Was this an equal treatment issue or an equal pay issue? The Court decided that it was not an equal treatment issue and stated:

> The answer to the first and fourth questions referred must therefore be that a sick-leave scheme which treats identically female workers suffering from a pregnancy related illness and other workers suffering from an illness that is unrelated to pregnancy comes within the scope of Article 141 EC and Directive 75/117.

The ECJ ruled that McKenna had not been treated unlawfully. It is interesting to note that in its judgment the Court rejected the findings of the Advocate General. The Court decided the issue on grounds of pay only. It stated:

> 1. A sick-leave scheme which treats identically female workers suffering from a pregnancy-related illness and other workers suffering from an illness that is unrelated to pregnancy comes within the scope of Article 141 EC and Council Directive 75/117/EEC of 10 February 1975 on the approximation of the

laws of the Member States relating to the application of the principle of equal pay for men and women.

2. Article 141 EC and Directive 75/117 must be construed as meaning that the following do not constitute discrimination on grounds of sex:

-a rule of a sick-leave scheme which provides, in regard to female workers absent prior to maternity leave by reason of an illness related to their pregnancy, as also in regard to male workers absent by reason of any other illness, for a reduction in pay in the case where the absence exceeds a certain duration, provided that the female worker is treated in the same way as a male worker who is absent on grounds of illness and provided that the amount of payment made is not so low as to undermine the objective of protecting pregnant workers;
- a rule of a sick-leave scheme which provides for absences on grounds of illness to be offset against a maximum total number of days of paid sick-leave to which a worker is entitled over a specified period, whether or not the illness is pregnancy-related, provided that the offsetting of the absences on grounds of a pregnancy-related illness does not have the effect that, during the absence affected by that offsetting after the maternity leave, the female worker receives pay that is lower than the minimum amount to which she was entitled during the illness which arose while she was pregnant.

Juries Act 1976
Section 29: places an obligation on an employer to allow his/her employees to attend for jury service, if called. Time spent on jury service is treated as time at work. Any person who is a citizen of Ireland and is between the ages of eighteen and seventy years whose name is on the Register of Electors may be called for jury service.

Ineligible persons
Certain persons are ineligible to serve on a jury. They include persons involved with the administration of justice, such as judges, former judges, practicing barristers, solicitors, court officers such as registrars and personnel in government departments involved in matters of justice or the courts, the President, the Attorney General, the Director of Public Prosecutions, members of An Garda Síochána, the Defence Forces and prison officers.

Disqualified persons
Persons living in Ireland who are not citizens are disqualified from jury service.

Persons who have been convicted of a serious crime in Ireland, or who have been sentenced, within the last ten years, to a term of imprisonment of at least three months, or those who have been sentenced to a term of imprisonment of five years or more are also disqualified from jury service.

Certain persons may be excused from jury service, including:
- persons between the ages of sixty-five and seventy;
- members of Dáil Éireann, the Seanad, the Council of State, the Comptroller and Auditor General, the Clerks of the Dáil and Seanad, a person in Holy Orders, a minister of any religious community, members of monasteries or convents, aircraft pilots, ships' masters and full-time students;
- persons providing a valuable community service, such as doctors, nurses, midwives, dentists, vets and pharmacists;
- persons who can certify that their duties cannot be performed by another person nor postponed, such as members of staff of the Dáil or Seanad, heads of Government Departments, civil servants, employees of local authorities, health boards and harbour authorities, teachers and lecturers;
- persons who have served on a jury within the previous three years or who have been excused by a judge at the conclusion of a previous period of service.

chapter 7

TERMINATION OF EMPLOYMENT

> This chapter will consider termination of employment through dismissal or redundancy.

Termination of a contract of employment may occur in a number of ways. An employer may dismiss for reason of redundancy or insolvency. A fixed-term contract may terminate by virtue of efflux of time. An employee may terminate employment by resigning voluntarily or s/he may terminate where, owing to circumstances, s/he feels there is no other option. The latter situation is known as constructive dismissal. It usually involves behaviour on the employer's part that, in essence, constitutes a repudiation of the contract of employment. It could include reducing remuneration or an adverse changing of work conditions.

The law governing termination is to be found in the following:
* Unfair Dismissals Acts 1977–2007 (Unfair Dismissals Acts 1977–1993, as amended by the Protection of Employees (Part-Time Workers) Act 2001;
* Protection of Employment (Exceptional Collective Redundancies and Related Matters) Act 2007;
* Industrial Relations Act 1969, as amended;
* breach of contract/wrongful dismissal.

Provisions are also to be found in a range of legislation covering, for example, employment equality, maternity protection, transfer of undertakings, adoptive leave, carer's leave, parental leave and health and safety leave.

• Unfair Dismissals Acts 1977–2007
The principal piece of legislation dealing with dismissal is the Unfair Dismissals Acts 1977–2001. This Act provides protection for employees against being unfairly dismissed from their employment by setting out criteria by which dismissals are deemed to be unfair or fair. It also provides redress for an employee whose dismissal is found to be unfair, namely reinstatement, re-engagement or a maximum of 104 weeks' remuneration.

Prior to the passing of this Act an employee had virtually no protection in law against arbitrary dismissal. If an employee considered that s/he had been unfairly dismissed, his/her only option was to pursue an action through the courts for wrongful dismissal, which was both a lengthy and an expensive process and clearly outside the range of possibility for most people. Industrial action was often the response to a dismissal notice and in 1975 it is estimated that one-third of days lost to disputes related to dismissals.

In 1993, during the legislative process of amending the Act, leading to the enactment of the 1993 Act, the Minister of State at the Department of Enterprise and Employment, commenting on the impact of the 1977 Act, stated:

> The proportion of [industrial disputes arising from unfair dismissal] as a percentage of all disputes has fallen from 20 per cent in 1976, the year before the introduction of the Act, to about 10 per cent a year since then and, in some years, the statistics has been as low as 7 or 8 per cent. This fact, taken in conjunction with the number of claims made under provisions of the Act, suggests that the Act has played a major role in reducing industrial relations tensions.
> (*Dáil Debates*, May 1993)

The Unfair Dismissals Acts 1977–2001 entitles employees covered under the Acts to bring a case to a Rights Commissioner or to the EAT in the event that they are unfairly dismissed. The case must generally be taken within six months of the date of dismissal.

Section 1: defines an *employee* as '*an individual who has entered into or works under (or, where the employment has ceased, worked under) a contract of employment*' and a *contract of employment* is defined as '*a contract of service or of apprenticeship, whether it is express or implied and (if it is express) whether it is oral or in writing*'.

In *John Sheridan v Fairco Ltd* UD684/2005 MN492/2005 the issue arose as to whether the claimant was an employee or not.

Facts: the claimant had worked as a sales representative for the respondent for four years. The respondent was a supplier and fitter of windows. The claimant was paid on a commission basis, drove his own car, paid for fuel and used his own mobile phone. The respondent provided him with a company business card and the samples and equipment he required for his work. His job was to conduct sales and to draw up sales contracts. He was responsible for the resolution of installation problems and would collect money from customers where the fitter had not done so. He attended trade shows for the company and worked regularly in their showrooms on Saturday mornings. He could not retain another person to do the company's work on his behalf. He worked solely for the company and was restricted from working for other companies that were in competition with the respondent. He received no payslips or P60s, but invoiced the company on a monthly basis in respect of his sales. There was no written contract between the parties. There was a signed declaration on the part of the claimant that he was being retained by the respondent.

The Tribunal referred to two Supreme Court cases in the course of its deliberations: *Henry Denny & Sons (Ireland) Ltd v Minister for Social Welfare* [1998] and *Castleisland Cattle Breeding v Minister for Social and Family Affairs* [2004]. The Tribunal noted that the Supreme Court held that consideration should not be confined to what was contained in a written contract of employment, but rather should have regard to all the circumstances surrounding the employment. A statement in a contract that a person is an independent contractor is not a contractual obligation, but merely a statement that might or might not be reflective of the actual legal relationship between the parties. The Tribunal was of the view that the opinions of the parties as to the nature and legal consequences of their relationship are not determinative.

The Tribunal accepted as appropriate in assessing the actual relationship between the parties guidance from Keane J. where, in the *Denny* case, he had stated:

> It is accordingly clear that while each case must be determined in the light of its particular facts and circumstances, in general a person will be regarded as providing his or her services under a contract of service and not as an independent contractor where he or she is performing those services for another person and not for himself or herself. The degree of control exercised over how the work is to be performed, although a factor to be taken into account, is not decisive. The inference that the person is engaged in business on his or her own account can be more readily drawn where he or she provides the necessary premises or equipment or some other form of investment, where he or she employs others to assist in the business and where the profit which he or she derives from the business is dependent on the efficiency with which it is conducted by him or her.

The claimant had made no investment in the respondent's business and had provided no premises. The equipment used was, in the main, the respondent's. The tasks carried out were not tasks that a sales representative would ordinarily undertake, but more the miscellaneous tasks in which an employee would engage. He was therefore working full-time for the respondent. The Tribunal held that the claimant was not performing the services for himself, but for the respondent, and was therefore an employee providing services under a contract of service.

This case is under appeal.

In a 2005 case the Employment Appeals Tribunal was asked to consider whether or not a rector was working under a contract of employment. The EAT held that he was not an employee:

> No contract of employment exists; the nature of the relationship cannot be analysed in contract terms because the Tribunal does not accept that there was an intention to create legal relations. The nature of the relationship with the church is that of a vocation or a calling which cannot be grounded in the common law notion of contract. [The rector's] duties are defined and his activities are dictated not by contract but by conscience.

In order for an employee to claim redress under the Unfair Dismissals Acts 1977–2001, s/he must have at least one year's continuous service with the employer. There are certain significant exemptions from this rule, such as where the dismissal results from:
- trade union membership or activity;
- pregnancy;
- maternity leave;
- adoptive leave;
- parental leave;
- carer's leave.

In such cases a claim can be brought regardless of length of service.

Employees Excluded from the Application of the Acts
Section 2: states that the Acts shall not apply to the following persons:
- an employee who has reached the normal retiring age for the employment in question. This should be interpreted in the context of the Equality Act 2004, which has removed the automatic exclusion of employees who have reached sixty-six years of age;
- persons working for a close relative in a private dwelling house or farm, provided both also live at that farm or house;
- members of the Defence Forces or An Garda Síochána;
- FÁS trainees and apprentices.

Civil servants were not covered by the Act until July 2006 when the Civil Service Regulations (Amendment) Act 2005 came into force. A new Civil Service Disciplinary Code was issued on the same day as the Act came into effect. The Code is concerned with disciplinary procedures relating to grades equivalent to principal officer and below. Disciplinary action may now be taken in cases of underperformance and may comprise formal notes on a personnel file, deferral of an increment, suspension and dismissal.

Types of Dismissal
Section 1: defines *dismissal* as:

> (a) the termination by his employer of the employee's contract of

employment with the employer, whether prior notice of the termination was or was not given to the employee

(b) the termination by the employee of his contract of employment with his employer, whether prior notice of the termination was or was not given to the employer, in circumstances in which, because of the conduct of the employer, the employee was or would have been entitled, or it was or would have been reasonable for the employee, to terminate the contract of employment without giving prior notice of the termination to the employer, or

(c) the expiration of a contract of employment for a fixed term without its being renewed under the same contract or, in the case of a contract for a specified purpose (being a purpose of such a kind that the duration of the contract was limited but was, at the time of its making, incapable of precise ascertainment), the cesser of the purpose.

Section 6: states that:

the dismissal of an employee shall be deemed, for the purposes of this Act, to be an unfair dismissal unless, having regard to all the circumstances, there were substantial grounds justifying the dismissal.

Dismissals are categorised under the Act as those that are fair (s 6(4)) and those that are unfair (s 6(2)).

Dismissals Automatically Deemed Unfair

Section 6(2) (as amended): provides that the dismissal of an employee will be deemed, for the purposes of the Act, to be an unfair dismissal if it results from one or more of the following:

(a) the employee's membership, or proposal that he or another person become a member of, or his engaging in activities on behalf of, a trade union or excepted body under the Trade Union Acts 1941 and 1971 [as amended by the Industrial Relations Act 1990], where the times at which he engages in such activities are outside his hours of work or are times during his hours of work in which he is permitted pursuant to the contract of employment between him and his employer so to engage,
(b) the religious or political opinions of the employee,
(c) civil proceedings whether actual, threatened or proposed

against the employer to which the employee is or will be a party or in which the employee was or is likely to be a witness,

(d) criminal proceedings against the employer, whether actual, threatened or proposed, in relation to which the employee has made, proposed or threatened to make a complaint or statement to the prosecuting authority or to any other authority connected with involved in the prosecution of the proceedings or in which the employee was or is likely to be a witness,

(dd) the exercise or proposed exercise by the employee of the right to parental leave or force majeure leave under and in accordance with the Parental Leave Act 1998 or carer's leave under and in accordance with the Carer's Leave Act 2001,

(e) the race, colour or sexual orientation of the employee,

(ee) the age of the employee,

(eee) the employee's membership of the Travelling community,

(f) the employee's pregnancy, attendance at ante-natal classes, giving birth or breastfeeding or any matters connected therewith,

(g) the exercise or proposed exercise by the employee of a right under the Maternity Protection Act 1994 to any form of protective leave or natal care absence, within the meaning of Part IV of that Act, or to time-off from work to attend ante-natal classes in accordance with s 15A (inserted by s8 of the Maternity Protection (Amendment) Act 2004) or to time-off from work or a reduction of working hours for breastfeeding in accordance with s15B (inserted by s9 of the Maternity Protection (Amendment) Act 2004) of the first mentioned Act,

(h) the exercise or contemplated exercise by an adoptive parent of the parent's right under the Adoptive Leave Acts 1995 and 2005 to adoptive leave or additional adoptive leave or a period of time off to attend certain pre-adoption classes or meetings.

In addition to the above, certain Acts have included protection against unfair dismissal for penalisation of an employee in relation to the exercising of rights under the legislation in question. The Safety, Health and Welfare at Work Act and the Employment Equality Acts are examples.

In *17 Complainants v Kilnaleck Mushrooms* UD155/2006 the issue of trade union membership arose.

Facts: the employees were migrant workers who were employed by the respondent as mushroom-pickers. They had been brought to Ireland for this specific purpose. In January 2006 they left their workplace owing to disputes concerning their work practices. They called to their local SIPTU office, which subsequently contacted the employer. They returned to work the following day to find they had been replaced. The respondent's assertion was that they had resigned as they had all walked out, leaving him to deal with an emergency situation of finding other people to pick the mushrooms. He also contended that they were not, in fact, employees, but self-employed contractors. Before the Tribunal hearing there was a Social Welfare finding that the employees had been in insurable employment with the respondent, and so this matter was not pursued by the respondent.

The Tribunal determined that the employees were dismissed because they had joined a trade union. The walk-out was a form of industrial action regarding work practices. The Tribunal described the dismissals as *flagrantly unfair* and noted that the claimants were all non-nationals with a limited command of English, many of whom had been brought to Ireland specifically to work at mushroom-picking. It went on to state:

> We are of the view that it would be just and equitable having regard to all the circumstances to make the maximum award in all cases.

In one of the highest awards ever made, the Tribunal awarded a total of €355,850—a maximum of 104 weeks' salary for each complainant.

Dismissals Deemed to be Fair
Section 6(4): provides that a dismissal will not be unfair if it results wholly or mainly from one or more of the following:

> (a) the capability, competence or qualifications of the employee for performing work of the kind which he was employed to do,
> (b) the conduct of the employee,
> (c) the redundancy of the employee, and
> (d) the employee being unable to work or continue to work in the position which he held without contravention (by him or by his employer) of a duty or restriction imposed by or under any status or instrument made under statute.

Section 6(6): '… *other substantial grounds*'.

Capability
Incapability was defined by the EAT in the case of *Reardon v St Vincent's Hospital* UD 74/1979 as follows:

> Incapability may be generally defined as long-term illness.

This would appear to mean that where an employee becomes unfit in the course of the employment to carry out the tasks for which s/he was hired, s/he may be dismissed and such a dismissal would be justified and therefore lawful.

In *Bolger v Showerings (Ire) Ltd* [1990] ELR 184, Lardner J. set out the requirements that an employer should comply with in order to justify a dismissal in such circumstances. This case concerned a forklift-driver who had a long history of absenteeism owing to ill-health. On three occasions the employee had been asked to have his doctor indicate a likely return-to-work date. In a reply from his doctor it was stated that the employee himself felt he would never be in a position to return to his previous job. The doctor also stated that the employee was due to be admitted to hospital for tests on his back. The employer had informed the employee that failure to provide a return-to-work date would result in dismissal on the grounds of incapacity. There was no dispute between the parties as to the incapacity. Mr Bolger was dismissed.

In an appeal before the High Court, Lardner J. stated:

> In this case it was the ill-health of the plaintiff which the company claimed rendered him incapable of performing his duties as a forklift driver. For the employer to show that the dismissal was fair, he must show that:
>
> (1) It was the ill-health which was the reason for his dismissal;
> (2) That this was the substantial reason;
> (3) That the employee received fair notice that the question of his dismissal for incapacity was being considered;
> (4) That the employee was afforded an opportunity of being heard.

A further point made in the case was quite significant and provided that where there was no dispute between the parties as to the incapacity due to ill-health, it was not necessary for the employer to await the results of medical tests before deciding to dismiss the employee. The court held in this case that the employer had substantial grounds for dismissal and the dismissal was deemed reasonable in all the circumstances.

It is well established that there is no obligation on an employer to provide alternative work or lighter duties for an employee who is no longer capable of performing his/her duties. This issue arose recently in *Carroll v Dublin Bus* [2005] IEHC 1. The plaintiff bus driver, employed by the defendant since 1995, was involved in a road accident in 2001. The following year he returned to work on a route that allowed him to get out of his seat regularly, as opposed to sitting in the driver's seat for significant continuous periods, as would be normal. In December

2002 he went on sick leave, claiming injury from a seat in the bus he was driving. Medical opinion was that he could return to work, but to a route that would allow frequent breaks. The employer's position was that no suitable route was available. Clarke J. reiterated the principle that there is no obligation on the employer to seek alternative work for the employer, but did add that:

> Such a position could, of course, be displaced by the existence of an express term, or perhaps a well established custom and practice amounting to a term of the contract.

It is possible that the doctrine of frustration could apply where the contract of employment ceases to bind the parties to it, if circumstances arise in which the contract becomes impossible of performance or in which performance of the contract is rendered radically different from that which was undertaken by the parties to the contract. Examples would be where an employee has suffered some serious injury or illness, or where the workplace premises has been destroyed. In *Gallagher v Eircom Ltd* UD 737/2003 an eight-year prison sentence was deemed to have automatically terminated the employment contract.

The area of incapacity is an extremely complex one. It should be noted that dismissing an employee on grounds of incapacity or ill-health may also come under equality legislation on the basis that the dismissal constitutes discrimination on the grounds of disability.

Competence
Competence concerns the employee's performance in his/her employment and the ability to carry out his/her duties. If there is an issue concerning an employee's competence, there are certain steps that *must* be taken by an employer *before* engaging in any action of a disciplinary nature. The employee must be given the opportunity to address the particular deficiency and must be told:
* what the deficiency is;
* what standard of performance is expected (this must be a reasonable standard);
* that the employee's performance is expected to improve and how (reasonable time must be given to achieve this);
* what the consequences of failure to improve will be.

If training is required, it should be provided. If failure to improve will lead to dismissal, the employee must be left in no doubt that this is the possible outcome of such failure.

Qualifications
Qualifications should rarely arise as a ground for dismissal. Issues may arise where the employee's original qualifications are no longer adequate for the performance

of the duties concerned. It is imperative in all such cases that the employer acts in a fair and reasonable manner.

O'Brien v CDVEC UD 959/1995

Facts: the claimant had been working as a part-time woodwork teacher, replacing a full-time teacher who was on sick leave. The person he was replacing resigned on grounds of ill-health and the post was advertised. The post was not filled. The claimant's qualifications did not meet the requirements set down by the Department of Education and Science, therefore he could not be appointed as a full-time teacher. He was, however, re-appointed in a part-time capacity. At the end of the academic year he was informed that he would not be re-employed the following year.

In a determination by the EAT, the Tribunal noted that the respondent was a passive party in the proceedings by reason of the restrictions placed on it by the Department of Education and Science. It went on to state:

> To employ any person in a capacity on a supposedly temporary contract for any period in excess of a year regardless of whether that person has knowledge of the temporary nature of the employment or not is in the Tribunal's opinion reprehensible and when this is combined then with a dismissal because they have found that that person does not satisfy particular requirements that they have arbitrarily set down even though those persons are actually fulfilling the day to day standards of a person in that post is in our opinion totally unreasonable.

Conduct

A good starting-point for any discussion on conduct in this context is Kenny J.'s proposition in *Glover v B.L.N. Ltd* [1973] IR 388, at p. 405:

> It is impossible to define the misconduct which justifies immediate dismissal ... There is no fixed rule of law defining the degree of misconduct which justify dismissal ... What is or is not misconduct must be decided in each case without the assistance of a definition or a general rule. Similarly, all that one can say about serious misconduct is that it is misconduct which the court regards as being grave and deliberate. And the standards to be applied in deciding the matter are those of men and not of angels.

In *Frizelle v New Ross Credit Union* [1997] IEHC 137, Flood J. considered a case of unfair dismissal and set down certain premises that must be established to support the decision to terminate employment for misconduct:

1. The complaint must be a bona fide complaint unrelated to any other agenda of the complainant.

2. Where the complainant is a person or body of intermediate authority, it should state the complaint, factually, clearly and fairly without any innuendo or hidden inference or conclusion.

3. The employee should be interviewed and his version noted and furnished to the deciding authority contemporaneously with the complaint and again without comment.

4. The decision of the deciding authority should be based on the balance of probabilities flowing from the factual evidence and in the light of the explanation offered.

5. The actual decision, as to whether a dismissal should follow, should be a decision proportionate to the gravity of the complaint, and of the gravity and effect of dismissal on the employee.

Put very simply, principles of natural justice must be applied unequivocally.

In *Frizelle* the plaintiff was employed as a manager of the defendant credit union from 1974. The credit union was a participant in a block fidelity and indemnity bond negotiated with an American insurance company called Cumis. The plaintiff was bonded under this policy. As part of the plaintiff's duties he had the power to approve secured loans up to the sum of £3,000 and unsecured loans up to the sum of £1,000. This he did under the supervision of the credit committee, which was provided with a record of each loan within seven days of the loan application. The committee was in turn obliged to report to the board of directors on a monthly basis.

The plaintiff purchased a house in 1988, and in 1992 decided to change it. When the sale fell through, the necessity for bridging finance arose. The defendant agreed to provide it. By January 1993 the first house remained unsold and the plaintiff had difficulty keeping up with the repayments. On 7 January 1993 he altered the computer file to re-phase the repayments to his account down to £165 per week. He did not inform anyone. This action was a non-authorised action by him. It did not reduce his financial liability to the defendants, but it did ensure that his account would not appear delinquent on the computer.

In a random check by the credit committee the re-phasing was discovered. Five of the six members of the committee advised the supervisory committee and the chairman of the board and requested a meeting of the board. It later emerged that some members of the board were at odds with some members of the credit committee.

The plaintiff was at no stage approached by the credit committee for an explanation. The meeting took place and became acrimonious, and the five members of the committee resigned. The plaintiff was excluded from this meeting.

Around this time a representative of the Irish League of Credit Unions was making a regular inspection. He noted a reference in the board's minutes to the plaintiff's unauthorised changes to his account. He reported this to Cumis, and as a result Cumis removed bonding from the plaintiff by endorsement of writing dated 8 March 1993. This decision meant that any action by the plaintiff as a member of staff of the credit union would not be bonded, therefore the credit union would be without indemnity of any kind and would be exposed. It also meant the plaintiff could no longer remain in the employment of the defendants. In subsequent correspondence it emerged that the basis on which the decision was made by Cumis was that:

> it is clear that this is a case of pre-meditated dishonesty and Cumis are not willing to bond Mr. Frizelle.

In the full plenary hearing of the case Flood J. noted that '*there was not one scintilla of evidence to justify anyone coming to the conclusion that there was any dishonest intent by the plaintiff in re-phasing his repayments*'. The loan had been repaid by February 1993. In a letter of 25 June his employment was terminated with regret.

Flood J. considered the actions of the five committee members. They had made a decision that there was dishonesty involved. This was not their function. It was their function to report to the board of directors. Further, it was their function and duty to seek an explanation from the plaintiff and to report that to the board. They did not do so. Flood J. was also of the view that the complaints about the plaintiff were part of a wider agenda. At no stage was the plaintiff afforded the opportunity to explain his side. *Per* Flood J.:

> In my opinion the whole procedure is so tainted with irregularity, impropriety, and other agenda, that this dismissal must be considered an unfair dismissal. In my view, having regard to all the circumstances, there was no substantial ground to justify dismissal.

Misconduct will usually refer to behaviour during the hours of employment. In some situations behaviour engaged in outside of working hours may be considered, if it relates in some way to the nature of the employment relationship. The dismissal of a doctor for a minor shoplifting conviction was held to be fair in *Shan v Croydon A.H.A* 13630/75/D (Eng.). In *Moore v C&A* [1981] IRLR 71 a store section leader was held to have been fairly dismissed for alleged shoplifting in another store. In *Caroline v Smith & Nephew Southhalls (Ire) Ltd.* UD

542/1984 it was held that the value of the product taken was irrelevant. A nurse was held to be fairly dismissed for the theft of a packet of cigarettes from a patient in *Dykyj v Barnet Area Health Authority* (1981) 24621/81/LN, and in *Brown v Portsmouth & S.E. Hampshire Health Authority* (1983) 21788/83 a kitchen superintendent's dismissal for stealing 50 pence worth of vegetables was held to be fair.

An employee who had worked for thirty-five years (fourteen with the respondent) and had an unblemished record was deemed to have been fairly dismissed in *Costello v Multiprint Labels Ltd* UD 55/2006. The claimant had been engaged in *double clocking* and was seen to do so on three occasions via CCTV cameras. Double clocking is a practice whereby an employee clocks another employee in or out of a premises when that employee is not on the premises. The practice constitutes fraud as the employee is being paid for time s/he has not worked. In the course of an investigation the claimant admitted that *double clocking* was wrong, but did not think it could lead to dismissal. The respondent had followed the company's disciplinary procedures and had carried out a proper investigation. The Tribunal held that the respondent had sufficient grounds to justify the dismissal.

In *Caffrey v The Belgard* UD 1150/2004 a security guard was dismissed on the ground of misconduct. The claimant had been with the company since 1987, providing security. The respondent claimed that the employee was intoxicated while on duty. This claim was denied by the employee, who said that he was simply tired from his long working hours and lack of sleep. There was conflicting evidence from witnesses as to whether or not he was under the influence of alcohol. At a meeting with the claimant a trade union representative expressed unease over the lack of relevant statements from witnesses being made available to him. The Tribunal determined that there was insufficient evidence to justify the dismissal. The Tribunal noted that the investigation carried out by the respondent was less than thorough.

Illustrating the point that even the most obvious case will fail if fair procedures are not followed is *McKenna v Butterly* UD 339/2006. This concerned an employee who had an arrangement with the company to take leave at short notice to accompany his sister to medical appointments. Suspicions arose among the joint managing directors that the arrangement was being abused when his colleagues commented during some of these absences that he was '*probably on the golf course again*'. On one occasion when he sent a text message to his foreman to say he would not be at work the next day, he was followed on the day in question and found to be on the golf course. He was subsequently dismissed for gross misconduct. However, owing to the unfairness of disciplinary procedures in the company, the EAT decided that the dismissal was unfair.

Loss of a driving licence rendering the employment impossible to continue would constitute a fair reason to dismiss: *O'Connor v Astra Pumps Ltd* UD 486/1986.

In the case of criminal activity outside the workplace, if there is a clear nexus with the employment, then there may be grounds for dismissal. In *Martin v Dunnes Stores (Enniscorthy)* UD 571/1988 the claimant was one of four defendants who, while under the influence of alcohol, broke into and stole from the premises of another retailer in the town. The offences were reported in a local newspaper. The dismissal was held to be fair as it constituted a serious breach of trust. In *Brady v An Post* UD 463/1991 the claimant was convicted of assault, but as he was held not to be in a position of special trust because he was employed as a cleaner his dismissal for the conduct was held to be unfair.

Mongan v C&D Foods Ltd UD 394/2005 Jan. 2007

Facts: this case arose as an appeal by the employee against a Rights Commissioner's recommendation. The employee had worked as a general operative with the employer since 2002. He suffered from literacy problems and the employer was aware of this situation. The employee was requested, by letter, to attend a disciplinary meeting and was given five days' notice. The letter warned of the possibility of dismissal. At no stage was he informed of specific allegations of wrongdoing, nor was he informed of a right to representation. The employee attended the meeting on 17 February and when asked to explain certain clocking-in discrepancies, he was unable to provide an explanation.

The Tribunal determined that the employer had failed to carry out a proper investigation of the matter. It had also failed to inform the employee of his right to appeal the decision to dismiss. The Tribunal overruled the Rights Commissioner's recommendation.

It is interesting to note that in its decision the employee's award reflected the fact that he had made no attempt to mitigate the loss resulting from the dismissal.

Redundancy

An employee's employment may be terminated by reason of redundancy where the employee's job is no longer available or because of a change in work practices. However, the redundancy must be a genuine one and the person selected must be selected in a fair manner. The onus is on an employer to justify the selection for redundancy.

Legislation covering redundancy is found in the Redundancy Payments Acts 1967–2003, as amended by the Protection of Employment Acts 1977–2003.

An employee who is dismissed, laid off or kept on short time for four or more consecutive weeks, or for a period of six or more weeks that are not consecutive but fall within a period of thirteen consecutive weeks, may be deemed dismissed by reason of redundancy if qualified under s 7(2).

Section 7(2) of the Redundancy Payments Act 1967, as amended, provides that a person who is dismissed shall be deemed to have been dismissed by reason of redundancy if the dismissal results *wholly or mainly* from one of the following five grounds:

> (a) the fact that the employer has ceased or intends to cease to carry on the business for the purposes of which the employee was employed by him, or has ceased or intends to cease, to carry on that business in the place where the employee was so employed, or
>
> (b) the fact that the requirements of that business for employees to carry out work of a particular kind in the place where he was so employed have ceased or diminished or are expected to cease or diminish, or
>
> (c) the fact that his employer has decided to carry on the business with fewer or no employees, whether by requiring the work for which the employee had been employed (or had been doing before his dismissal) to be done by other employees or otherwise, or
>
> (d) the fact that his employer has decided that the work for which the employee had been employed or had been doing before his dismissal) should henceforward be done in a different manner for which the employee is not sufficiently qualified or trained, or
>
> (e) the fact that his employer has decided that the work for which the employee had been employed (or had been doing before his dismissal) should henceforward be done by a person who is also capable of doing other work for which the employee is not sufficiently qualified or trained.

Note the grounds outlined are not purely economic in nature.

A case where the definition of *redundancy* was considered was *St Ledger v Frontline Distribution Ltd* [1995] ELR 160:

> Redundancy has two characteristics which are of importance in this case. It is impersonal and it involves change.
>
> It is impersonal in the sense that it does not relate to something the employee has done wrong in the workplace, rather the redundancy impacts on the job and not the person. Only as a

consequence of the redundancy does the employee involved lose the job. The change referred to means change in the workplace. It may include a complete closedown, a reduction in the need for employees or a reduction in numbers, a change in the way the work is done or some other change in the nature of the job.

The Redundancy Payments Acts oblige employers to pay compensation to employees dismissed by reason of redundancy. In order to be protected by the Acts an employee must satisfy the following requirements:
- be aged between sixteen and sixty-six years;
- have worked for the employer on a continuous basis for 104 weeks prior to being made redundant;
- be in insurable employment within the meaning of the Social Welfare Acts.

The Acts: provide that where an employee's period of service is interrupted by a period of not more than twenty-six consecutive weeks by reason of holidays, lay-offs or any cause other than the voluntary leaving of his/her employment, continuity of employment shall not be broken.

An employer should have an agreed redundancy procedure that sets out the objective criteria that would justify one employee being chosen for redundancy over another. An important case in relation to the selection issue is *Williams v CompAir Maxam Ltd* [1982] IRLR 83, where a set of procedures was suggested for reasonable employers faced with the task of selecting employees for redundancy:

> There is a generally accepted view in industrial relations that, in cases where the employees are represented by an independent union recognized by the employer, reasonable employers will seek to act in accordance with the following principles
>
> 1. The employer should give as much warning as possible to enable the union and employees to inform themselves of the relevant facts, consider or find alternative solutions or employment.
>
> 2. The employer should consult with the union as to the best means to effect the redundancy with as little hardship to the employees as possible. Agreement on selection criteria should be agreed.
>
> 3. Criteria used for selection should be objectively verifiable and should not depend solely on the opinion of the person making the selection. Attendance record, efficiency at the job, experience or length of service should be used.

4. The selection should be based on these criteria. Any representations from the union should be considered.

5. The employer should consider the possibility of alternative employment in the company.

Under the Protection of Employees (Part-Time Work) Act 2001 and the Protection of Employees (Fixed-Term Work) Act 2003, part-time and fixed-term employees may not be treated less favourably than comparable full-time employees in the absence of objective grounds.

Other Substantial Reason (Justifying Dismissal)
In *Flynn v Power* ([1985] IR 648) a teacher in a Catholic school was dismissed because she was living with a married man and had become pregnant by him, conduct described as *fundamentally inconsistent* with her position as a teacher in the school. The appellant claimed that her private life was her own. The court held that the appellant was employed in a religious, not a lay, school with long established and well-known aims and objectives, as well as the requirements for its lay staff, which are different from those of a secular institution. The dismissal was not for a breach of a code of conduct, but arose from an assessment that a continued breach would damage the school's efforts to foster in their pupils norms of behaviour and religious tenets that the school had been established to promote. The appellant's relationship with the married man was carried on openly and publicly in a country town with quite a small population. In such circumstances the school had substantial grounds for dismissal.

Procedures
Section 7(a) is quite significant and provides that the Rights Commissioner, Tribunal or Circuit Court hearing a case or the appeal of a case and in determining whether the dismissal of an employee was an unfair dismissal may consider:

(a) the reasonableness or otherwise of the conduct (whether by act or omission) of the employer in relation to the dismissal.

In *State (Gleeson) v Minister for Defence and Attorney General* [1976] IR 210, Walsh J. stated that:

To the right to work may be added the right to continue to earn a livelihood which can be taken away or forfeited only if the procedure followed is clearly lawful. Hence lawfulness of procedures or basic fairness of procedures is due, it may be argued, to all employees under the Constitution.

A case where the EAT considered in detail what constituted fair procedures in a dismissal situation is *Pacelli v Irish Distillers Ltd* UD 571/2001 EAT. It was a case concerning suspected misconduct in the workplace.

Facts: the claimant had worked for the respondent for twenty-nine years and at the time of his dismissal had been engaged for twenty years in loading delivery trucks at the respondent's bottling plant. By 2000 he was a supervisor and was responsible for checking loads. During 1999 and 2000 the company experienced serious stock losses and carried out a series of investigations. Employees were questioned as part of the investigation, video cameras were installed and a private investigator was employed. Evidence was discovered of overloading of delivery trucks, bogus deliveries to non-customers and interference with locks to the warehouse.

Meetings were held with the claimant on 5 and 12 April 2001, at which he was asked about his involvement in overloading, interference with counters and possible intimidation. He could offer no explanation. The human resources director was present at these meetings. The claimant was suspended on full pay on 12 April. There was a further meeting on 17 April and the following day he was dismissed because it was felt there was a complete breach of trust.

In considering what amounts to fair procedures in a dismissal case, the Tribunal referred to a number of cases.

In *Bunyan v UDT (Ire) Ltd* [1982] ILRM it was held that:

> ... the fairness or unfairness of the dismissal is to be judged by the objective standard of the way in which a reasonable employer in those circumstances in that line of business would have behaved. The Tribunal therefore does not decide whether or not, on evidence before it, the employee should be dismissed. The decision to dismiss has been taken and our function is to test such decision against what we consider the reasonable employer would have done and/or concluded.

Noting that all employees are entitled to fairness of procedures irrespective of their standing in an organisation, the Tribunal referred to *Gunn v National College of Art and Design* [1990] 2 IR, where Walsh J. stated that:

> The application of these rules (natural justice) does not depend upon whether the person concerned is an office-holder as distinct from being an employee of some other kind ... The quality of justice does not depend on such distinctions ...

The Tribunal continued to state that in any dismissal case it is a prerequisite to conduct an investigation and that '*such investigation should have regard to all the facts, issues and circumstances surrounding a case warranting serious chastisement or reprimand, such as dismissal*'.

According to the Tribunal, the crux of this case concerned the actual investigation of the matters complained of, the conclusions reached by the employer and whether the employer had an honest belief or a suspicion of the claimant's involvement. The Tribunal was satisfied that the investigation by the respondent was thorough and fair in the circumstances. As the claimant featured in a number, if not all, occasions of questionable happenings and practices within the precinct of the company warehouse, namely:

- stock losses occurring on his shift;
- case-counter failing to record transactions accurately;
- the placing of two cases parallel to each other on a conveyor-belt, forcing the electronic counter to record them as one case;
- locks on certain gates being interfered with;
- deliveries to non-customers and non-deliveries to certain customers;
- interference with the closed circuit camera monitoring system;
- overloading of trucks;
- company product going missing,

> ... it is nothing short of sheer torture of logic to suggest that the claimant has not at least a case to answer.

The Tribunal accepted that where an officer of a company suspects unusual conduct is occurring amounting to malpractice, criminal activity or unacceptable behaviour, s/he may question the person(s) with a view to identifying the offender/s:

> ... questioning itself cannot be said to implicate the party being questioned as that party has an obligation to the company to assist it with its enquiries. Employees have a duty to assist management in their investigations.

In this case the Tribunal noted the unhelpfulness of the claimant during the course of the investigation. When asked about the issue of overloading and the delivery to a private residence who was not a customer, his response was that any evidence the company had was *hearsay* and that was *no evidence*. Evidence was outlined to the claimant of the number of boxes of product that had been overloaded and it was stated that, notwithstanding this, all procedures seemed to be in order. The claimant's response was *you prove it* and that the investigation was some type of *kangaroo court*. He stated that the company had no proof to attach any blame to him, however the Tribunal was of the view that it did not require such proof but rather a reasonable suspicion that the claimant had a case to answer. The Tribunal concluded that the claimant's conduct and the position he adopted at the interviews could be described as less than helpful, on the one hand, and total defiance, on the other.

The Tribunal also noted that it was not its function to say whether or not the claimant was in fact guilty of any or all of the happenings. The matter for consideration was much narrower than that, *viz. did the respondent company act fairly, properly and justly in reaching its decision to dismiss the claimant?* The test for *reasonableness* was set out in *Noritake (Irl) Ltd v Kenna* (UD 88/1983):

1. Did the company believe that the employee mis-conducted himself as alleged? If so,
2. Did the company have reasonable grounds to sustain that belief? If so,
3. Was the penalty of dismissal proportionate to the alleged misconduct?

On this test the Tribunal found that the respondent acted fairly and having regard to the grave nature of the misconduct the penalty was proportionate thereto.

In *Neill Ryan v Window Blinds Manufacturing Ltd* UD 1430/2005 the Tribunal held that the claimant had been unfairly dismissed. The claimant was a general operative with the respondent. It was submitted by the respondent company that the claimant had been late seventy-six times and absent for forty-six days. The first absence took place in February 2005. There was disagreement between the parties as to verbal warnings given. The respondent claimed to have given twelve verbal warnings over the late arrivals at work, while the claimant denied ever having received them. The Tribunal held that the claimant had been unfairly dismissed and awarded compensation. The company had no policy dealing with absenteeism, the claimant had not been asked to explain the sick leave and the warnings given regarding the time-keeping were inadequate.

The issue of suspension from employment came up for consideration in *Allman v Minister for Justice & A.G* [2003] ELR 7. The case concerned two prison officers who had been escorting a prisoner on day release. Arising out of an altercation at a licensed premises in which both officers had been involved, the prisoner had to return to prison unaccompanied by either officer. Allegations were made that the officers had allowed the prisoner to move freely without their constant supervision. The officers were suspended from duty. Disciplinary proceedings were commenced, but as it was a flawed process, the employer proposed to set aside the first hearing and to hold a second hearing in 2000. At this stage judicial review was sought by the applicants of the decision to hold a hearing three-and-a-half years after the alleged incident. The applicants argued that their constitutional rights had been breached and that the respondents had failed to comply with the principles of natural and constitutional justice and fairness of procedures. Referring to the Supreme Court decision in *Flynn v An Post* [1987] IR 68, Kearns J. accepted that:

> the process or power of suspension must be construed in employment circumstances as permitting a suspension to continue only for such a period of time as may be necessary or reasonably practicable to have a full hearing into the matter giving rise to the suspension, so as to determine whether the employee be dismissed, reinstated or dealt with in some other way.

Reinstatement with full pay and full allowances was awarded from January 2000, the date up to which it was accepted that the suspensions had been valid.

• Constructive Dismissal

Section 1 of the 1977 Act defines *constructive dismissal* as:

> the termination by the employee of his contract of employment with his employer whether prior notice of the termination was or was not given to the employer in circumstances in which, because of the conduct of the employer, the employee was or would have been entitled or it was or would have been reasonable for the employee to terminate the contract of employment without giving prior notice of the termination to the employer.

The core issue in constructive dismissal is, therefore, that the employee is forced to leave his/her job because of the unreasonable behaviour or conduct of the employer, or that the employer has breached the contract of employment. In a constructive dismissal case the onus is on the employee to prove that the employer's behaviour was unreasonable in the circumstances and that s/he had no alternative but to resign from the job. As a general rule, the employee must be seen to have acted reasonably.

O'Connell v Dunnes Stores UD885/2005, MN 649/2005

Facts: in an accident twenty years earlier the claimant had injured the tendons of the two middle fingers of his right hand. As a result, his fingers were extremely sensitive and he was unable to handle small objects without considerable discomfort. When he was transferred to a job that involved using a till and handling small coins, he requested a move and indicated a willingness to work in any other department. His request was not facilitated and he felt he had no option but to resign, which he did. His claim of constructive dismissal was successful. The EAT found that the respondent had acted unreasonably in its failure to give any consideration to his disability when they transferred him to a department where his work involved the use of tills and the handling of small coins.

It is worth noting that in this case the claimant could have gone the route of bringing a discrimination claim on the grounds of disability to the Equality Tribunal under the Equality Acts.

A leading case in this area is *Allen v Independent Newspapers* UD641/2000

Facts: the claimant was employed by the *Sunday Independent* as a crime reporter. She claimed she was subjected to continuous harassment and bullying by both colleagues and management and that she was isolated to such an extent that her confidence and health had been undermined. Details were given of the change to her work as a crime correspondent, whereby she was asked to write a social column with the newspaper. Her flexible working conditions were changed. There was hostility in the workplace. Rumours circulated about persons being recruited to work in her area. She could not tolerate her working environment and was left with no other option but to resign. There was medical evidence that the difficulties she was experiencing were caused by her work situation.

The EAT found that the claimant had been constructively dismissed and as there was no evidence offered to rebut the presumption of unfairness, the Tribunal determined that she had been unfairly dismissed. Her decision to resign had been reasonable in the circumstances. On the question of a remedy, it was accepted that re-employment was not a feasible option in the situation, leaving compensation as the only available remedy. However, there was the question of whether an award could be made where an employee was unavailable for work due to illness attributable to the actions of the employer. In cases where an employee is unfit for work, it may be argued that no loss flows from the dismissal and therefore no compensation attaches. The Tribunal held that her illness was attributable wholly to the factors that had led her to resignation. Her illness had led to her financial loss and this financial loss was attributable to the conduct of the respondent.

> To hold otherwise, in light of the findings made, would in the view of this Tribunal, have the effect of leaving an unfairly dismissed employee (where re-instatement or re-engagement have been ruled out as unsuitable remedies) without any effective remedy for the financial loss suffered as a result of the dismissal. Such a result would in our view be contrary to the intention and spirit of Section 7 of the Unfair Dismissals Act.

Remedies

An employee unfairly dismissed under the Act is entitled to redress. Section 7 of the 1977 Act as amended states:

> (a) reinstatement by the employer of the employee in the position which he held immediately before his dismissal on the terms and conditions on which he was employed immediately

before his dismissal together with a term that the reinstatement shall be deemed to have commenced on the day of the dismissal; or

(b) re-engagement by the employer of the employee either in the position which he held immediately before his dismissal or in a different position which would be reasonably suitable for him on such terms and conditions as are reasonable having regard to all the circumstances

(i) if the employee incurred any financial loss attributable to the dismissal, payment to him by the employer of such compensation in respect of the loss (not exceeding in amount 104 weeks remuneration in respect of the employment from which he was dismissed calculated in accordance with regulation under s17 of this Act) as is just and equitable having regard to all the circumstances, or

(ii) if the employee incurred no financial loss, payment to the employee by the employer of such compensation (if any, but not exceeding in amount 4 weeks remuneration in respect of the employment from which he was dismissed calculated as aforesaid) as is just and equitable having regard to all the circumstances.

Reinstatement

Reinstatement means, in essence, that the employee who has been unfairly dismissed is reinstated in his/her old position, effective immediately. It is as though the employee was never dismissed. It is usually awarded where there is no blame attributable to the employee. The employee is entitled to any arrears of salary, which includes all benefits. Reinstatement will not usually be awarded where the relationship of trust has broken down between the parties.

In *Moore v Xnet Information Systems & Others* [2002] 2 ILRM 278 the High Court held that reinstatement pending the hearing of the case would not be granted as relations between the parties had broken down irretrievably and the balance of convenience did not therefore favour reinstatement.

In *Wernstrom v Galway Aviation Services Ltd* UD 1460/2004 the Tribunal asked the employer to consider reinstatement, but if it that was not possible, then compensation would be awarded.

Facts: the employee was a pilot in the respondent's company. Two incidents occurred that resulted in the claimant being summarily dismissed. The first incident concerned a flight approach that was described as having been executed in a careless manner. After the incident the claimant was called to a meeting with the operations manager and told that he would have to improve if he wished to hold onto his job. The second incident occurred when the claimant taxied the plane over an object on the runway and damaged a fuel pump. The pilot was dismissed. The operations manager stated that he no longer had confidence in the claimant and that he could not allow the employee to operate company aircraft.

The Tribunal considered the procedures adopted by the company in the case. The claimant had not been informed that the meeting with the operations manager was a disciplinary one. In a subsequent meeting where he was told he was to be dismissed, he asked to have a solicitor present and was informed that he could not get one at such short notice. He was at no stage asked to explain his actions in the two incidents complained of. The Tribunal concluded that the summary dismissal had been inappropriate and procedurally unfair. There should have been a proper investigation. The claimant was awarded compensation.

Re-Engagement
Re-engagement provides that the employee is re-employed either in the same job or in an appropriate or reasonably suitable different job on such terms and conditions as are reasonable, having regard to all the circumstances.

Compensation
The maximum amount of compensation payable to an employee who has been unfairly dismissed is 104 weeks' remuneration. Compensation will be for actual loss, as well as for future losses. Actual losses include salary, annual bonus, employer's contribution to a pension scheme, annual value to the claimant of the private use of the company car, employee's PRSI and state pension contribution, plus the value of lunches and subscriptions: *Bunyan v United Dominions Trust (Ire) Ltd* [1981] ILRM 404.

For the loss to be compensated it must be attributable to the dismissal. Section 7(1)(c)(i) provides that:

> if the employee incurred any financial loss attributable to the dismissal, payment to him by the employer of such compensation in respect of the loss (not exceeding in amount 104 weeks remuneration in respect of the employment from which he was dismissed calculated in accordance with regulations under s 17 of this Act) as is just and equitable having regards to all the circumstances.

Injunction
An injunction is an order by a court that either prohibits a person from performing a particular act or requires that person to carry out a particular act. One of the first cases where an injunction was used was *Fennelly v Assicurazioni Generalli SPA Ltd* [1985] I.L.T.R. 73. The plaintiff had resigned from An Garda Síochána to work as an insurance claims assessor for the defendant company. He

claimed that he had been given a fixed-term contract for twelve years. The employer gave notice of its intention to terminate the employment, arguing that owing to a downturn in business there was no position for Mr Fennelly. Until the matter could be heard the employer was directed to pay the plaintiff's salary.

Injunctions can only be granted by a court.

Industrial Relations Act 1969
An employee with less than one year's service may bring a claim under this Act. Such claims will go to the Labour Relations Commission and a conciliation officer or to a Rights Commissioner and, on appeal, to the Labour Court. In general, awards are lower.

Employment Equality Acts 1998–2004
If an employee believes s/he was discriminated against on any of the prohibited grounds in the Acts, s/he may bring a claim of discrimination to the Equality Tribunal for the dismissal. The maximum award under this legislation is two years' remuneration.

References
On termination of employment, particularly where it arises from the voluntary resignation of the employee, the question of references may arise. There is no general obligation on an employer to provide an employment reference. The leading case in this area is the UK case of *Spring v Guardian Assurance* [1994] (House of Lords).

Facts: Mr Spring worked with a company that was sold on to Guardian Assurance. The person appointed as chief executive did not get on with Mr Spring and he dismissed him without explanation. Mr Spring and another person sought to go into business selling insurance for another firm. Under the rules of the Life Assurance and Unit Trust Regulatory Organisation (LAUTRO), it was not possible to be appointed as a representative of a company unless the company satisfied itself as to character and competence, including seeking a reference. A reference was sought from his former employer.

The reference received from Guardian Assurance included the following comments:

> ... he was seen by some of the sales staff as a person who consistently kept the best leads for himself with little regard for the sales team that he supposedly was to manage; and his former superior has further stated that he is a man of little or no integrity and could not be regarded as honest ...

The other company declined to appoint him. Two other companies approached also declined to appoint him. He subsequently brought an action against his former employer on a number of grounds, including negligent misstatement, malicious falsehood and breach of contract.

Lord Woolf stated:

> The duty imposed by the Lautro Rules is not for the protection of employees. It is for the protection of the public. An employee cannot therefore rely on the rules directly. However, they nonetheless demonstrate the importance now attached in the insurance industry to references being given and obtained. To be of value they need to be full, frank and, by implication, accurate references.

The question for the Law Lords in the case was '*whether one who supplies a defamatory reference about a person in response to a request from a concern with which that person is seeking employment is liable in negligence to the subject of the reference if it has been compiled without reasonable care*'.

It was held by a majority that an employer who gives a reference in respect of a former employee owed that employee a duty to take reasonable care in its preparation. That employer could be liable in negligence if s/he failed to do so and the employee suffered economic loss as a result. It was likened to the duty to protect an employee from physical injury. Though this case only has persuasive authority in this jurisdiction, it will be relied on by employees in similar situations. It should be noted that the *Spring* case is unusual in that, because of industry rules, there was an obligation on an employer to provide a reference.

In a subsequent UK Court of Appeal case, *Bartholomew v London Borough of Hackney* [1999] 246, which built on the *Spring* case, the Court stated that an employer had a duty of care to provide a reference that was true, accurate and fair.

In an Irish case, *TSB Bank v Harris* [2000] IRLR 157, an employer who supplied a reference that was misleading and unfair was held by the EAT to be in breach of the implied term of trust and confidence. The reference had outlined complaints against the employee of which she had been unaware and consequently provided a misleading impression of her.

In addition to negligence, a former employee could bring an action for defamation.

Retirement Age

There is no mandatory retirement age under Irish law. It is a contractual matter to be set down by an employer in the conditions of employment. In the absence of a retirement age being set down, an employer may not terminate a person's employment on the basis that s/he has reached a particular age.

Section 34(4) of the Employment Equality Acts 1998–2004 provides that:

> … it shall not constitute discrimination on the age ground to fix different ages for the retirement (whether voluntarily or compulsorily) of employees of any class or description of employees.

In October 2007 the ECJ handed down an important case relating to retirement age. *Palacios de la Villa v Cortefiel Servicios SA* concerned a State's (Spain) right to set mandatory retirement ages. The Court held that it was in order for a State to set a mandatory retirement age of sixty-five years as the measure could be objectively and reasonably justified in the context of national law by a legitimate aim relating to employment policy in the labour market. Spain was using the mandatory retirement at sixty-five as a measure to reduce unemployment amongst under-sixty-fives. As it was being used to exercise control of the labour market, it could be objectively and reasonably justified. Accordingly, the Court held:

> The prohibition on any discrimination on grounds of age, as implemented by Council Directive 2000/78/EC of 27 November 2000 establishing a general framework for equal treatment in employment and occupation, must be interpreted as not precluding national legislation such as that at issue in the main proceedings, pursuant to which compulsory retirement clauses contained in collective agreements are lawful where such clauses provide as sole requirements that workers must have reached retirement age, set at 65 by national law, and must have fulfilled the conditions set out in the social security legislation for entitlement to a retirement pension under their contribution regime, where
>
> – the measure, although based on age, is objectively and reasonably justified in the context of national law by a legitimate aim relating to employment policy and the labour market, and
>
> – the means put in place to achieve that aim of public interest do not appear to be inappropriate and unnecessary for the purpose.

In light of this decision it may be the case that the setting of mandatory retirement age may be open to challenge.

Collective Redundancies

One example of the effect of the legislative changes committed to by the Irish Government under the Social Partnership Agreement *Towards 2016* is the Protection of Employment (Exceptional Collective Redundancies and Related Matters) Act 2007. The Irish Ferries dispute in 2005, which resulted from the company's decision to replace 543 permanent unionised crew with agency workers sourced in eastern Europe, who were to be paid considerably lower wages, provided the impetus for this legislation. Also in 2005 was the case of *Junk v Kuhnel* 2005 IRLR 310, where the ECJ held that there was an obligation on employers to consult prior to deciding to terminate contracts of employment. The effect of this was to prolong the period between the start of a redundancy process and implementing those redundancies.

Until 2007 collective redundancies were covered by the Protection of Employment Act 1977. A collective redundancy refers to dismissals effected in any period of thirty consecutive days of:
- at least five employees, where the workforce is between twenty and fifty employees;
- ten employees, where the employees number between fifty and 100;
- 10 per cent of employees, where the employees number between 100 and 300;
- thirty employees, where over 300 are employed.

Under that Act an employer was obliged to give information to representatives of employees likely to be affected by proposed redundancies and to the Minister for Enterprise, Trade and Employment, and also to enter into consultations with the representatives. Redundancies could not take place until a thirty-day period had elapsed from the commencement of the process.

Exceptional collective redundancies under the 2007 Act are dismissals where:
- the dismissal is one of a number of dismissals that together constitute collective redundancies (as described above);
- the dismissals are compulsory;
- the dismissed employees were, or are to be, replaced at the same location or elsewhere in the State (except where the employer has an existing operation with established terms and conditions) by –
  (a) other persons who are, or are to be, directly employed by the employer, or
  (b) other persons whose services are, or are to be, provided to that employer in pursuance of other arrangements;
- those other persons perform or are to perform essentially the same functions as the dismissed employees; and
- the terms and conditions of employment of those other persons are, or are to be, materially inferior to those of the dismissed employees.

Section 4: provides that this does not apply to the employment of agency workers for temporary or recurring business needs or to the use of outsourcing, or other forms of business restructuring.

Section 12: provides that '*Consultations under this section shall be initiated at the earliest opportunity and in any event at least 30 days before the first notice of dismissal is given*'.

Section 5: sets up a Redundancy Panel that will comprise a Chairperson appointed by the National Implementation Body and a member appointed by the Irish Congress of Trade Unions (ICTU) and the Irish Business and Employers' Confederation (IBEC), each member having a deputy.

Where a collective redundancy is proposed, the employer or the employees' representatives may refer the circumstances to the panel for consideration on whether the redundancies constitute an exceptional collective redundancy. There are strict time limits within which this must be done. The panel informs the Minister for Enterprise, Trade and Employment and also invites the parties to make submissions. The panel may either request the Minister to seek an opinion from the Labour Court or may express the view that certain preconditions to the panel's determinations have not been met. The Minister may make a request to the Labour Court for an opinion. There is no appeal from the Labour Court.

If the Labour Court's view is that it is an exceptional collective redundancy and the employer proceeds with the dismissal, the consequences are serious:
- the employer may be denied the statutory rebate of 60 per cent;
- the income tax exemption that usually applies to statutory redundancy will not operate;
- claims brought by employees under the Unfair Dismissal Acts could find that the threshold of the awards are increased.

chapter 8

EQUALITY

> This chapter will consider the law on equality and look at the origins of that law and the legislation giving it effect.

Any discussion on the subject of equality in the workplace in Ireland must be framed within the context of our membership of the EU. Ireland's decision to join the European Communities, which became effective in January 1973, led to profound changes in the law, affecting equality in pay and conditions of employment. Upon joining, Ireland accepted the dominance of European law over its own existing domestic law.

The origin of the law on equality is to be found in the Treaty of Rome and, in particular, in Art 119 (now Art 141). Article 119 provides:

> Each Member State shall during the first stage ensure and subsequently maintain the application of the principle that men and women should receive equal pay for equal work.
> For the purpose of this Article, 'pay' means the ordinary basic or minimum wage or salary and any other consideration, whether in cash or in kind, which the worker receives, directly or indirectly, in respect of his employment from his employer.
>
> Equal pay without discrimination based on sex means:
> (a) that pay for the same work at piece rates shall be calculated on the basis of the same unit of measurement;
> (b) that pay for work at times shall be for the same job.

It is not without significance that the only reference to equal treatment in the Treaty is in the context of pay. More motivated by the desire to ensure that no one Member State's employers had a competitive advantage over another than concern over the unfair treatment of women, it nonetheless had a profound impact on the issue of equality. France had enacted laws in 1957 that were favourable to workers but more costly to employers and therefore could be perceived as having placed France at an economic disadvantage compared with other Member States. Equal pay for men and women formed part of those laws. To protect French industry from unfair competition from other Member States where female workers did not enjoy equal pay, Art 119 was included in the Treaty. Ireland sought a derogation from Art 119 on economic grounds, but was not successful.

It was not until the 1970s that Art 119 and the principle of equal pay found true legal expression. That came about in the case of *Defrenne v Sabena* 43/75 [1976] ECR, in which the ECJ stated:

> the aim of Article 119 is to avoid a situation in which undertakings established in States which have actually implemented the principle of equal pay suffer a competitive disadvantage in intra-Community competition as compared with undertakings established in States which have not yet eliminated discrimination against women workers as regards pay. Secondly, this provision forms part of the social objectives of the Community, which is not merely an economic union, but is at the same time intended, by common action, to ensure social progress and seek the constant improvement of the living and working conditions of their peoples, as is emphasized by the Preamble to the Treaty.

The claimant in the *Defrenne* case was a former air-hostess with the Belgian national airline, Sabena, who had lodged claims with the Belgian courts relating to equal pay and equal pension entitlements. Unlike male stewards, who performed the same work as their female colleagues, air-hostesses were forced to retire at the age of forty. Ms Defrenne brought a claim before a Belgian court alleging discrimination contrary to Art 119 of the Treaty in respect of loss of salary, loss of severance pay and reduced pension resulting from her compulsory retirement at age forty.

Her employer, Sabena, did not dispute that the work done by male stewards and female air-hostesses was identical nor that there was discrimination in terms of pay. The matter was referred to the ECJ. The claimant asserted that she was entitled to equal pay with her male colleagues during a period of time when there was no Belgian legislation in force on equal pay, that period being February 1963 to February 1966.

In a landmark decision the Court held that the principle of equal pay for equal work flowing from Art 119 was directly enforceable, irrespective of the enactment of the implementing legislation. It was sufficiently precise to enable individuals to rely on it directly before a national court. It therefore applied in Member States from their dates of accession to the Community.

It is interesting to note that the governments of Ireland and the UK made an intervention before the Court, on economic grounds, fearing the effect of the right to equal pay being declared retrospective to the time of joining and the impact this might have in each State. Ireland had passed the Anti-Discrimination (Pay) Act in 1974, but it had not come into effect until December 1975. Ireland joined the EEC in 1973. If Art 119 had direct effect, then Irish female workers could have claims predating the national legislation and stretching back to 1973—the date of Ireland's accession. It was argued successfully by Ireland that the immense financial burden in meeting such claims would undermine the economic stability of the State. The estimated cost was put at IR£40 million. The Court did acknowledge the difficulties posed by such a decision for the UK and Ireland and consequently limited the retroactivity of the decision. The Court decided that the direct effect of Art 119 could be relied on only by those claims relating to pay periods after the date of the *Defrenne* judgment, unless such proceedings had already been initiated.

Not only was the decision important from the point of the substantive issue of equal treatment but it was also far-reaching in terms of the integrative effect of Community law. The Court's concern was to ensure that the Community's aims were given effect.

The *Defrenne* decision was of major importance because it established the principle that Art 119 had direct effect. Furthermore, not only did it apply directly to each Member State but in each State it gave rights to individuals that were enforceable against the State and other individuals. The Article was therefore said to have both *vertical and horizontal effect.*

• Anti-Discrimination (Pay) Act 1974

Though passed in 1974, this Act did not come into operation until December 1975. The purpose of the Act was to give effect to Art 119 of the Treaty: '*An Act to ensure equal treatment, in relation to certain terms and conditions of employment, between men and women employed on like work.*' The Act provided that where a man and a woman were employed in the same place, by the same employer or associated employer, and they were doing *like work*, then they should receive the same remuneration. It implemented Directive 75/117 on the approximation of the laws of the Member States relating to the application of the principle of equal pay for men and women

• Employment Equality Act 1977

Following on from the 1974 Act came the first Equality Act in 1977, which made illegal any discrimination on grounds of sex or marital status. This Act was designed to protect male as well as female workers. It was enacted on foot of Directive 76/207 on the implementation of the principle of equal treatment for men and women in relation to access to employment, training, promotion and working conditions. The Employment Equality Agency was established under this Act.

Today, the principal Acts concerned with the issue of equality are the Employment Equality Act 1998, the Equal Status Act 2000 and the Equality Act 2004.

- ## Employment Equality Act 1998 (as amended by the 2004 Act)
The Employment Equality Act 1998 (as amended in 2004), which came into effect in October 1999, repealed the Anti-Discrimination (Pay) Act 1974 and the Employment Equality Act 1977.

Section 6 of the 1998 Act outlaws discrimination on the following nine grounds:
- gender;
- marital status;
- family status;
- sexual orientation;
- religion;
- age;
- disability;
- race;
- membership of the Traveller community.

Section 6, as amended by s 4 of the 2004 Act: provides that *discrimination*, for the purposes of the Act, occurs where:

> (a) one person is treated less favourably than another person is, has been or would be treated in a comparable situation on any of the discriminatory grounds which
>> (i) exists
>> (ii) existed but no longer exists
>> (iii) may exist in the future, or
>> (iv) is imputed to the person concerned
>
> (b) a person who is associated with another person
>> (i) is treated, by virtue of that association, less favourably than a person who is not so associated is, has been or would be treated in a comparable situation, and
>> (ii) similar treatment of that other person on any of the discriminatory grounds would, by virtue of (a), constitute discrimination.

This s 4 definition is a broader definition than the original s 6 definition, which provided that discrimination occurs where, in respect of the nine discriminatory grounds, *'one person is treated less favourably than another is, has been or would be treated'*. Discrimination may take a number of forms, including indirect discrimination, discrimination by imputation and discrimination by association. It includes the issue of an instruction to discriminate.

Discrimination on the gender ground includes discrimination related to pregnancy or maternity, where a woman employee is treated less favourably for those reasons.

Section 8 of the 2004 Act, amending s 14: holds that harassment and sexual harassment constitute discrimination in relation to the victim's conditions of employment.

Less favourable treatment may relate to unequal pay for like work, but may also relate to specific areas, as set out in s 8:
- access to employment;
- conditions of employment;
- training or experience for or in relation to employment;
- promotion, re-grading or classification of posts;
- dismissal;
- collective agreements;

It provides that an employer '*shall not discriminate against an employee or prospective employee and a provider of agency work shall not discriminate against an agency worker*'.

Like work is defined as work that is the same, similar or work of equal value. Equal pay claims may be taken on any of the nine discriminatory grounds.

The Act applies to:
- full-time, part-time and temporary employees in the public sector;
- prospective employees;
- vocational training bodies;
- employment agencies;
- trade unions, professional and trade bodies;
- self-employed;
- partnerships;
- persons employed in another person's home.

Gender
The ground of gender is concerned with the status of a person as being a man or a woman. The 2004 Act amended this definition so that it now includes pregnancy or maternity leave. Discrimination will have taken place on the gender ground if a woman is treated less favourably because of pregnancy than another employee is, has been or would be treated.

In the case of *Maye v ADM Ringaskiddy* DEC E2006-004 the issue of pregnancy arose.
Facts: the claimant alleged that she had been treated less favourably than other employees because of her pregnancy. When she notified her employer of her pregnancy, she also informed them of her inability to do night work or heavy duties. This was supported by medical certification. She was immediately put on health and safety leave. She was informed that there was no suitable alternative

work available that did not pose a risk and that her employer could not create work for her owing to financial difficulties. On the intervention of her union she was provided with light daytime duties for a six-week period. It was argued that on another occasion an employee had been placed on light duties. The Equality Officer held that there had been discrimination on the grounds of gender when she had received less favourable treatment because of her pregnancy. The respondent had failed to satisfy the Equality Officer that it had made a genuine effort to find alternative work for her. She was awarded €8,000 in compensation and €5,981 for loss of earnings.

Ms BH v A name Company t/a A Cab Company DEC E2006-026
Facts: the complainant worked in the base office of a taxi company. She claimed that several incidents occurred in 2002 and 2003 that amounted to her being discriminated against by the respondent on grounds of gender. Incidents referred to included the following:

- dead fish had been thrown onto an internal roof of the office directly affecting her work area. Noxious smells had resulted from the company's failure to remove the fish;
- remarks overheard which indicated an underlying intention to sexually harass;
- laxative tablets and steroids were placed in the office kettle, aimed at her, she alleged, because of her gender and weight;
- grossly offensive and humiliating pictures, one of which had her name on it, were displayed in the office.

The complainant alleged these activities were directed at her not only because of gender but also because she was in a gay relationship. She made a number of complaints to the company, but she alleged nothing was done in response. The respondent accepted that the incidents did occur, though it did take place under previous management, and it argued that the actions of a handful of drivers did not mean that there was an anti-female bias in the company. It acknowledged that there was no policy on the matter in place in the company. The Equality Tribunal was satisfied that sexual harassment had taken place

The Equality Tribunal noted s 23 of the 1998 Act, where it states that sexual harassment by an employee, employer or, subject to certain conditions, in a business contract constitutes discrimination by the employer on the gender ground in relation to the employee's conditions of employment.

Perhaps contrary to popular perception, cases on gender grounds are not taken exclusively by women, as the following case will illustrate.

In *Dunnes Stores v O'Byrne* the issue concerned the refusal of a male employee to wear a face mask or to shave off his beard. He was dismissed. Initially he was told to keep his beard neatly trimmed, but was later requested to shave it off completely. Neither the complainant nor fellow employees were required to cover head hair while at work. On appeal to the Labour Court, the Court held that a dress code should apply a common standard of neatness, conventionality and hygiene to both men and women and it should not unreasonably bear more heavily on one gender than on the other. The Court ordered the employee's reinstatement from the date of dismissal without loss of pay.

Employers have the right to impose dress restrictions on employees, but the employer should be able to demonstrate that the restriction is reasonable and not discriminatory.

Marital status
The ground of marital status relates to a person's status as single, married, widowed, separated or divorced. *NBK Designs v Inoue* ED/02/34 0212 is a case where gender, family status and marital status were raised.

Facts: the complainant was a part-time secretary/personal assistant who job-shared with another person. During 2001 a decision was taken to convert the two part-time positions to a single full-time post. The complainant was asked to take on this new post. Owing to her childcare responsibilities, which were known to the respondent, she was unable to work on a full-time basis and advised the company accordingly. She was given four weeks' notice of dismissal. The complainant contended that the requirement to work full-time was a condition of employment that disadvantaged significantly more women than men and significantly more of her marital and family status than people of a different marital and family status. She was a lone parent.

There were two issues for determination, in the opinion of the Court. First, could the requirement to work full-time be complied with by a significantly higher proportion of men than women and/or those of a different marital or family status from that of the complainant? If the answer was in the affirmative, then the requirement was *prima facie* discriminatory. Secondly, the Court must then go on to consider if the requirement could be justified by objective factors unrelated to the complainant's gender. The Court found, as a general proposition, that women who have children and are single, separated or divorced find it more difficult to work full-time than fathers who are single, separated or divorced, or men who are not parents. The Court was satisfied that there was indirect discrimination. On the question of whether there was objective justification for the discrimination the Court found none:

> On the evidence before it the Court is far from convinced that
> the exigencies of the respondent's business made it essential that
> the complainant work full-time.

An award of €10,000 in compensation was made.

Family status
The ground of family status refers to a person's role or responsibility as a parent of a person under eighteen years of age, a parent with a disabled child or being a resident primary carer. The case of *Gaelscoil Thulach na Nog v Markey* ED/04/1 EED049 illustrates this ground.

Facts: the facts of this case concerned a school secretary who claimed she was dismissed on grounds of her family status and religious belief. The complainant had three children attending the school at the time. Difficulties arose in the school around the introduction of a new religious education programme, which the principal was refusing to implement. The complainant publicly supported the principal in this stance. There was also an alleged breach of confidentiality concerning her terms of employment, which had been discussed at a Board of Management meeting. On foot of a letter of complaint the principal was directed to investigate the matter and she was requested to retract and make an apology. This matter escalated, resulting in an exchange of solicitors' letters. At a meeting of the Board of Management a decision to dismiss her from her position was taken and a letter to that effect was delivered to her house. The respondent stated the reason for the dismissal as follows: '*it was inappropriate to have as Secretary to the school a person who was at the same time a parent of a child in the school*'.

It went on to say that the decision was directly related to the controversy at the school regarding the religious education programme and took the view that there could be a conflict of interest in the future between a person's duty as a parent and a duty to the school. The Board also contended that it had lost trust and confidence in the complainant as a result of the decision that the confidentiality complaint was unfounded.

The Labour Court found that the claimant was discriminated against on the ground of family status. As a parent of a child under the age of eighteen she was subject to less favourable treatment than a person without children would have been. On the religious ground the Court did not make a finding of discrimination, believing that the controversy over the new religious programme did not have any bearing on the Board's decision to dismiss.

As relations between the parties had broken down completely, reinstatement or re-engagement were not appropriate remedies, therefore compensation was awarded.

Sexual orientation
The ground of sexual orientation relates to a person's status as being homosexual, bisexual or heterosexual. It should be noted that very few cases have been taken on this ground. In *Piazza v Clarion Hotel* DEC-E2004-033 discrimination on the ground of sexual orientation was raised by the complainant.

Facts: the dispute centred on a number of incidents that it was alleged constituted harassment, whereby reference was made to the complainant's sexual orientation in a degrading manner. In an email from one manager to the HR manager he was referred to as *'just a bloody woman and a spoilt child'*. In another incident he was called a *'gay bastard'* in the presence of other members of staff. The Equality Officer was satisfied that these incidents constituted harassment and could reasonably be regarded, in relation to his sexual orientation, as offensive, humiliating or intimidating to him. She went on to find that though there was a grievance policy in the company, it was not sufficiently detailed to indicate how such a matter could be progressed. An investigation had been carried out, but the outcome was unsatisfactory in the Equality Officer's view in that no findings were communicated to the complainant, no apology was given, no message was issued that such behaviour was unacceptable and no sanction was imposed for the conduct complained of. The respondent also appeared to attach blame to the complainant.

The issue of vicarious liability was raised. Section 15(1) of the 1998 Act provides:

> Anything done by a person in the course of his or her employment shall, in any proceedings brought under this Act, be treated for the purpose of this Act as done also by that person's employer, whether or not it was done without the employer's knowledge or approval.

As the acts complained of were carried out by the employees in the course of their employment, the employer was vicariously liable for those actions. It is a defence under s 32(6) for an employer to show that reasonably practicable steps were taken to prevent the harassment taking place. The Equality Officer was satisfied that no policy on the prevention of harassment was in existence at the time, therefore this defence could not be availed of by the employer. The Equality Officer found that the respondent had discriminated against the complainant on the sexual orientation ground. The complainant was awarded €10,000 and the respondent was ordered to redraft its Respect and Dignity policy and communicate it to relevant staff and to provide equality training for all staff.

Religion

In *Ahmed v ICTS (UK) Ltd* EDA043 the issues of both race and religion were raised.

Facts: the case concerned a complainant who was a Sudanese national and a member of the Muslim faith and a respondent pan-European company, based in the UK, providing security to certain airlines operating out of Dublin Airport. The complainant alleged that at his interview for a job as a security agent he was subjected to questions and comments that were disparaging of his race and religion. The respondent denied the allegations, stating that the complainant may have misunderstood the interviewer when he was explaining the nature of the job. The respondent denied asking the complainant if he was Muslim. The claim that a question was asked about terrorist attacks in Sudan was also denied. The respondent stated that the interview commenced with an explanation of what the job entailed, why it was being done and the emphasis placed on security in the wake of the Lockerbie tragedy—the biggest airline tragedy to have occurred close to Dublin. The bulk of the respondent's work, it submitted, was to limit the risk of terrorist attack to clients' assets. The questions asked in relation to passport details and status in Ireland were asked of all applicants for security and legal reasons.

The respondent submitted that the complainant produced a bundle of papers that he said were letters of rejection from other employers and stated that all Irish employers were racist. The claimant stated that he became angry at the interview, threw his application form in the nearest bin and left. It was noted by the Equality Officer that in the original submission no reference was made by the complainant to a question on religion, yet in the second submission he alleged that it was the second question asked. The respondent submitted it operated an equal opportunities policy and employed eighty staff at Dublin, representing eight different nationalities.

The Labour Court, on appeal from the Equality Officer's decision, upheld that decision and found that the complainant did not establish a prima facie case of discrimination.

Age
The age ground applies to all ages above the statutory school-leaving age. An interesting case taken on the age ground was *Vickers v Daughters of Charity of St Vincent de Paul* DEC-E2007-017.

Facts: in this case the claimant alleged discrimination on grounds of age when she was obliged to retire against her will on the last day of her sixty-fifth birthday. The claimant had been employed since 1992 by the respondent under a Community Employment Scheme that was funded by FÁS. Her contract was renewed annually. Her employment with the respondent was under the provisions of the scheme and was contingent on funding from FÁS. When the complainant reached the last day of her sixty-fifth birthday, FÁS ceased funding her on the Community Employment Scheme, in accordance with the rules of the scheme.

> In line with Government policy, participation on employment schemes has an upper age limit of 65 years of age i.e. FÁS may provide funds to community based employers to cover participant costs until the day before their 66th birthday (at which point entitlement to a state pension becomes available).

When funding ceased, the respondent could no longer retain the complainant in its employment.

The Court noted s 34(4) of the Act:

> ... it shall not constitute discrimination on the age ground to fix different ages for the retirement (whether voluntary or compulsorily) of employees or any class or description of employee.

It concluded that the respondent was not enforcing a discriminatory policy of another organisation. The respondent did not itself have a mandatory retirement age and its policy was that retirement was determined by an employee's capability and performance. The respondent had no difficulty with the complainant's capability and performance, but it was prevented from retaining her in the absence of funding from FÁS. Accordingly, the Court found that in the dismissal the respondent had not discriminated against the complainant on grounds of age.

Disability

The ground of disability is concerned with a broad range of disabilities, including physical, intellectual, learning, cognitive, or emotional disability.

Section 1 defines *disability* as:

> (a) the total or partial absence of a person's bodily or mental functions, including the absence of a part of a person's body
> (b) the presence in the body of organisms causing, or likely to cause, chronic disease or illness
> (c) the malfunction, malformation or disfigurement of a part of a person's body
> (d) a condition or malfunction which results in a person learning differently from a person without the condition or malfunction, or
> (e) a condition, illness or disease which affects a person's thought processes, perception of reality, emotions or judgement or which results in disturbed behaviour,
> and shall be taken to include a disability which exists at present, or which previously existed but no longer exists, or which may exist in the future or which is imputed to a person.

In *A Government Department v an Employee* EDA062 the complainant, a senior civil servant, alleged discrimination on the grounds of disability.

Facts: a recovering alcoholic had been employed as a HEO since 1979 and was the longest serving HEO in the Department. Though initially his work performance and self-confidence had been affected by his alcoholism, these had shown a marked improvement with the treatment he had commenced in 1995. The complainant applied unsuccessfully to be placed on a panel for a number of promotions in 2000, 2001, 2002 and 2003. In 2004 he was successful, but no vacancies were filled from the panel. In 2005 he again applied to be included, but was unsuccessful. He alleged that his lack of success was due to his alcoholism.

The respondent contended that alcoholism was not a disability and further that as the complainant had not consumed alcohol since 1995, he was no longer suffering from alcoholism. It was also contended that alcoholism was not a factor in the decision not to include him on the panel, but rather it was concerns about his ability to represent the Department at external meetings.

The Equality Officer found that there had been discrimination on the grounds of disability. The respondent appealed that decision and the matter came before the Labour Court.

The Court held that alcoholism was a disability within the meaning of the Act. It further held that the respondent had discriminated against the complainant on the grounds of disability and ordered the respondent to appoint the complainant to the relevant post and to backdate pay. An award of €6,000 in compensation was also ordered to be paid.

Some noteworthy issues were highlighted by the Court in the course of its deliberations in the case. It noted that no minutes were maintained of meetings where decisions were made in respect of a candidate's suitability to be placed on a promotional panel. There were no records of criteria used. The Court ordered that the respondent introduce measures to ensure that the promotions process be conducted in a transparent fashion thereafter.

The duty to make a reasonable accommodation for staff with a disability has arisen in a number of cases. The case described below was an appeal against a decision of the Equality Tribunal, in which it was found that the respondent had discriminated against a civil servant on the disability ground. The case came before the Labour Court as *A Government Department v An Employee (Ms B)* ADE/05/16 061.

Facts: the claimant was a clerical officer who was assigned to a department in 1990. She suffered from a serious eye condition that was a disability within the meaning of the Act. As a result of this condition she was unable to use a VDU, and so performed manual functions only. When first assigned to her post her disability had a limited effect on her capacity to carry out the full range of clerical officer duties. In 1994, however, the Department became fully computerised and the complainant became confined to a progressively restricted range of manual duties and tasks, which continued to diminish over time. The respondent had asked the complainant's optician about the possibility of providing the complainant with a large VDU, but the optician had advised against it. No other steps were pursued to find ways that the complainant might be more fully involved in the work of the department.

In November 2002 a vacancy arose for a staff officer, a promotional grade, at the complainant's office. The post was to be filled by the most senior suitable candidate. The complainant was the most senior candidate. The process of selection required the complainant's manager to assess her suitability for promotion. The manager concluded that the complainant did not have the necessary qualities or knowledge for promotion. In the absence of a favourable report, the claimant could not be appointed to the post. The claimant contended that she was not promoted because of her disability. The respondent disputed this, stating that the reason for not recommending her for promotion was performance-related and unrelated to her disability. These issues had never been formally raised with the complainant. An agreement existed between the respondent and a trade union representing civil servants that where it was apprehended that an officer's performance might be such as to render him/her unsuitable for promotion, s/he would be notified not later than twelve months before s/he would be considered for promotion. The complainant was never informed that there was an issue with her performance that impacted on her suitability for promotion.

Referring to s 16 of the Act, the Court noted that the prohibition on discrimination on grounds of disability is not absolute:

> S16(1): Nothing in this Act shall be construed as requiring any person to recruit or promote an individual to a position, to retain an individual in a position, or to provide training or experience to an individual in relation to a position, if the individual
> (a) will not undertake (or, as the case may be, continue to undertake) the duties attached to that position or will not accept (or, as the case may be, continue to accept) the conditions under which those duties are, or may be required to be, performed
> (b) is not (or, as the case may be, is no longer) fully competent and available to undertake, and fully capable of undertaking, the duties attached to that position, having regard to the condition under which those duties are, or may be required to be, performed.

Section 16(3): goes on to state that a person with a disability is regarded under the Act as being fully competent and fully capable of undertaking any duties '... *if with the assistance of special treatment or facilities, such person would be fully competent to undertake, and be fully capable of undertaking those duties*'. Note that in the 2004 Act this was amended and now requires '... *appropriate measures to be provided by the employer,* rather than *special treatment or facilities*'. Such measures should not impose a *disproportionate burden* on the employer. What remains unchanged is that the employer must make a *reasonable accommodation* of the person's needs. That accommodation now applies to access to employment as well as participating in, advancing in and undergoing training in a workplace. Appropriate measures could include adaptation of equipment or premises, changing working time patterns, redistributing tasks or providing training.

The Court commented:

> The scope of an employer's duty is determined by what is necessary and reasonable in the circumstances. It may, as in the instant case, involve relieving the person with a disability from the requirements to undertake certain work which is beyond his or her capacity. However if this results in a diminution of the person's prospects of advancement in employment it would seem reasonable to conclude, on a purposive construction of the Section, that the employer should then consider if any countervailing measures could be taken to ameliorate that disadvantage.

The Court concluded that the difficulties in finding useful work for the complainant and her resulting failure to gain the experience commensurate with her length of service were as a result of her disability. The respondent had failed to consider, in consultation with the complainant, alleviating measures that might have been put in place to offset this disadvantageous situation. Neither did the respondent inform the complainant of any issues it had in respect of her performance. The Court found in favour of the complainant, thereby affirming the Equality Officer's decision, and ordered an award of €10,000. It also directed the respondent to put in place training for relevant staff pursuant to its obligation to provide reasonable accommodation to staff members with a disability.

A wide range of disabilities have come before the Equality Tribunal, including cerebral palsy, anorexia, bulimia, arthritis, diabetes, schizophrenia and many more.

Race
Race is defined as including colour, nationality or ethnic origin. An important case in relation to recruitment and selection procedures is the Equality Tribunal case of *Czerski v Ice Group* DEC-E2006-027. It is also concerned with the issue of indirect discrimination.

Facts: the claimant alleged discrimination on grounds of gender and race by the respondent employment agency in relation to access to employment following an interview with one of the respondent's clients in August 2001. The complainant had replied to an advertisement for a Production Operative, a position she was holding in another company at the time, which company was experiencing a downturn in business. Two employment-related references were required. The complainant was only able to supply one, from her current employer, because she had been at home rearing her family between 1986 and 2000 and before that she was employed in Poland. At a subsequent interview no mention was made of any problems with references. She was informed that there were no vacancies at that time, but that her name would be kept on file. When a number of her colleagues were subsequently recruited by the company, she telephoned the respondent to enquire why she had not been selected for one of the posts. It was at this stage, she argued, that the issue of the failure to provide two references was raised. She also alleged that she was informed that only men were being recruited as the post involved heavy lifting.

This allegation was disputed by the respondent. The respondent stated that in the absence of a second reference, it had no option but to inform the complainant that no suitable employment was available.

The Equality Officer rejected the claim of discrimination on gender grounds, believing that the claimant was told that the position involved heavy lifting rather than a statement that only men were being recruited. On the question of the reference requirement, the Equality Officer noted the Service Agreement the respondent had with the potential employer, which stated that *'two career references will be checked prior to starting with APC'*. The Equality Officer concluded that this requirement operated to the disadvantage of a non-Irish national as compared with an Irish national. He went on to say:

> I am further satisfied that the requirement could be complied with by a substantially smaller number of prospective employees who are non-Irish nationals as compared to prospective employees who are Irish nationals. Consequently, I find that the complainant has established a prima facie case of indirect discrimination on grounds of race.

It could be said that the difficulties posed by such a requirement could act equally against nationals who, for reasons of disability or child-rearing, found themselves outside the workforce for a number of years. A requirement that a potential employer will only accept work-related references has the potential to discriminate against a wide number of potential candidates. Providing a character reference should be considered an acceptable alternative.

Membership of the Traveller community
This concerns a person's status as a Traveller, a person identified by Travellers and others as having a shared history, culture and traditions that is nomadic on the

island of Ireland. This ground was considered in *Maguire v North Eastern Health Board* DEC-E2002/039.

Facts: the complainant alleged discrimination on the Traveller ground when he was treated differently by management and staff after they discovered he was a Traveller and his complaint in respect of harassment at a Christmas party was not investigated. The complainant commenced employment with the respondent as a temporary care attendant in November 2001. Three weeks into working with the respondent, he alleged, attitudes towards him changed. This followed a fellow worker having recognised him from schooldays. The complainant attended the staff Christmas party, at the end of which a fellow worker invited staff back to her house to continue the festivities and allegedly said in his hearing, '*the knacker is not coming*'.

The respondent denied the allegation of less favourable treatment and stated that the reason for not dealing with the harassment complaint was that as the incident occurred outside the workplace, it was not appropriate to get involved. The Equality Officer noted the 2002 Code of Practice (Harassment) Order, S.I. No. 78, where it states:

> The scope of the sexual harassment and harassment provisions extend beyond the workplace for example to conferences and training that occur outside the workplace. It may also extend to work-related social events.

The Equality Officer was satisfied that the Christmas party was related to work. The complainant would not have been present at the party if he had not been employed by the respondent. According to the respondent, there were a number of complaints about his work and despite warnings there was no improvement, hence the decision to terminate his employment. This was not accepted by the Equality Officer because there was evidence that the complainant had been asked to sign a contract of employment a number of days before he made the complaint. He had been rostered to work five days per week up to the time of the complaint following the Christmas party, but thereafter his working time was reduced significantly from five to two days.

The Equality Officer found that the complainant had been discriminated against on the Traveller ground and also that he had been victimised. An award of €5,000 was made and the respondent was ordered to implement a harassment policy, a code of practice on staff treatment of members of the Travelling community and to implement a transparent disciplinary policy.

Sexual Harassment

Section 8 of the 2004 Act introducing a new s 14A to the 1998 Act defines harassment as:

> … any form of unwanted conduct related to any of the discriminatory grounds.

Sexual harassment is defined as:

> … any form of unwanted verbal, non-verbal or physical conduct of a sexual nature.

In both cases it is conduct that has the '*purpose or effect of violating a person's dignity and creating an intimidating, hostile, degrading, humiliating or offensive environment for the person*'. The unwanted conduct may consist of acts, requests, spoken words, gestures or the production, display or circulation of written words, pictures or other material.

The harassment or sexual harassment prohibition concerns such offending behaviour from another employee, the employer, clients, customers or other business contacts of the employer with whom the employer might reasonably expect the victim to come into contact, and where the circumstances of the harassment are such that the employer ought reasonably to have taken steps to prevent it or to reverse the effects of it. An Equality Tribunal case worth noting in this regard is *Ms Z v A Hotel* DEC–E2007-014. The case concerned the alleged sexual harassment of an employee and discriminatory treatment in that she was not re-engaged by the respondent after a period of lay-off.

Facts: the complainant commenced work as a casual part-time waitress with the respondent in October 2004. On the night of 7 December she attended the respondent's Christmas party in the company of a friend and work colleague, Ms X. The complainant alleged that at around 3.00am Mr A, the General Manager of the hotel, who was sitting alone at the time, beckoned her to sit beside him. He proceeded to tell her she looked gorgeous that evening, that he wanted to go home with her and that they should get a taxi together. She contended that he repeated this a number of times, although he did not touch her in an inappropriate manner. She submitted that this behaviour constituted sexual harassment contrary to the Employment Equality Acts 1998 and 2004. She further alleged discriminatory treatment when, early in the New Year, there was a lay-off of staff and she was not re-engaged.

The complainant's version of the events that had taken place at the party was roundly rejected by the respondent, who submitted that it was the complainant's behaviour that was inappropriate in that she had made advances to him.

The complainant referred a complaint to the Equality Tribunal under the 1998 and 2004 Employment Equality Acts and an Equality Officer was directed to investigate the complaint.

The Acts (s 85A) set out the burden of proof necessary in claims of discrimination. It requires the complainant to establish, in the first instance, facts from which it can be inferred that she was sexually harassed and treated less favourably on the ground cited. It is when she has discharged this burden to the satisfaction of an Equality Officer that the burden shifts to the respondent to rebut the inference of discrimination raised. *Sexual harassment* is defined in the Act as:

> Any form of unwanted verbal, non-verbal or physical conduct of a sexual nature, being conduct which has the purpose or effect of violating a person's dignity and creating an intimidating, hostile, degrading, humiliating or offensive environment for the person.

Evidence given to the Equality Officer was contradictory and she therefore had to decide, on balance, which version was the more credible. The complainant's version was accepted as the more credible. It was also decided that the comments did fall within the definition of sexual harassment.

As the harassment took place at the Christmas party, could it be construed as having occurred in the workplace or in the course of the complainant's employment? The Employment Equality Act 1998 (Code of Practice) (Harassment) Order 2002 was cited. It states:

> The scope of sexual harassment provisions extend beyond the workplace for example to conferences and training that occur outside the workplace. It may also extend to work related events.

The Christmas party was deemed to be work-related insofar as the complainant would not have been present if she had not been employed by the respondent.

It was noted that s 14A provides a defence for the respondent in cases of sexual harassment in that it is a defence for the employer to prove that reasonably practicable steps were taken to prevent harassment. In this instance there was no policy, written or verbal, in operation in the workplace. There was no established complaints procedure. The respondent could not, therefore, rely on the defence.

The finding was in favour of the complainant and the following order was made:

(1) The respondent was ordered to pay €12,000 by way of compensation for the distress and effects of the discrimination and harassment.
(2) A Code of Practice to be developed on all nine grounds covered by the Acts within three months of the decision.
(3) That the Code be given to all existing staff and new staff on

joining. Copies with brief synopses should be displayed prominently in the areas of the hotel frequented by staff.

(4) That all staff with management functions receive appropriate training and that such training be reviewed routinely in light of developments and best practice in the area.

Vicarious Liability

Section 15 of the 1998 Act provides that an employer is vicariously liable for anything done by an employee in the course of his/her employment, whether or not it was done with the employer's knowledge or approval. It is a defence for the employer if it can be proven that the employer took such steps as were reasonably practicable to prevent the employee from doing the acts complained of.

Victimisation

Section 29 of the 2004 Act, amending s 74 of the 1998 Act, prohibits victimisation of employees. Victimisation occurs where an employee is dismissed or is otherwise treated adversely by the employer as a reaction to an employee:

- making a complaint of discrimination to the employer;
- taking proceedings against the employer;
- representing or supporting a complainant;
- being a comparator or a witness for the purposes of the Act;
- opposing acts which are unlawful under the Act;
- giving notice of an intention to take any of the actions mentioned above.

Equal Pay

Section 19 of the Act provides for equal pay for like work. *Like work* is defined in s 7 as the same or similar work or work of equal value. Equal pay claims may be brought on any of the nine discriminatory grounds. It is an implied term in all contracts of employment that there is an entitlement to equal pay.

A controversial decision in the area of equal pay was the ECJ's decision in *Cadman v Health and Safety Executive* C-17/05. The case concerned a female employee in the HSE in the UK and whether length-of-service increments were contrary to gender equality.

Facts: Ms Cadman argued that an automatic link between length of service and higher pay operated to the detriment of female workers, who were more likely to have absences from the workplace for family reasons and therefore shorter length of consecutive service than male colleagues. Ms Cadman lodged an application before the Employment Tribunal under the Equal Pay Act (UK). At the time of her claim she had been in a managerial post for nearly five years. She took as comparators four male colleagues who were in the same category as her. They had longer service than Ms Cadman, part of which had been acquired in more junior posts, and they were being paid substantially more than her.

The Tribunal held that the term in her contract relating to pay should be modified so as not to be less favourable than that in the employment contracts of her four comparators. The HSE appealed that decision to the EAT. That Tribunal held that, based on the ECJ decision in the 1988 *Danfoss* case 109/88, where unequal pay arose because of the use of length of service as a criterion, no special justification was required. This decision was appealed to the Court of Appeal by Ms Cadman.

The matter came before the Court of Justice by means of a Preliminary Ruling reference from the Court of Appeal. The Court was uncertain as to whether the *Danfoss* case had been departed from, therefore a preliminary ruling was sought from the Court of Justice. The following questions were referred:

> 1. Where the use by an employer of the criterion of length of service as a determinant of pay has a disparate impact as between relevant male and female employees, does Article 141 EC require the employer to provide special justification for recourse to that criterion? If the answer depends on the circumstances, what are those circumstances?
> 2. Would the answer to the preceding question be different if the employer applies the criterion of length of service on an individual basis to employees so that an assessment is made as to the extent to which greater length of service justifies a greater level of pay?
> 3. Is there any relevant distinction to be drawn between the use of the criterion of length of service in the case of part-time workers and the use of that criterion in the case of full-time workers?

Article 141 lays down the principle that equal work or work of equal value must be remunerated in the same way:

> Each member State shall ensure that the principle of equal pay for male and female workers for equal work or work of equal value is applied.

Article 1 of Council Directive 75/117 states:

> In particular where a job classification system is used for determining pay, it must be based on the same criteria for both men and women and so drawn up as to exclude any discrimination on grounds of sex.

The Court of Justice held that the first and second questions must be answered as follows:

-Since as a general rule, recourse to the criterion of length of service is appropriate to attain the legitimate objective of rewarding experience acquired which enables the worker to perform his duties better, the employer does not have to establish specifically that recourse to that criterion is appropriate to attain that objective as regards a particular job, unless the worker provides evidence capable of raising serious doubts in that regard.

-Where a job classification system based on an evaluation of the work to be carried out is used in determining pay, there is no need to show that an individual worker has acquired experience during the relevant period which has enabled him to perform his duties better.

The third question did not need to be answered in light of the answers given to the first and second questions.

Advertising posts

Section 10: prohibits job advertisements that could reasonably be interpreted as indicating an intention to discriminate. With the change in definition of *indirect discrimination* introduced by the 2004 Act, indirect discrimination now arises where an apparently neutral rule or provision puts people in a particular category, e.g. age or other ground, at a particular disadvantage in respect of any matter when compared with fellow employees or prospective employees. If the provision is objectively justified by a legitimate aim and the means of achieving that aim are appropriate and necessary, then it may not constitute discrimination.

In *Equality Authority v Ryanair* DEC-E/2000/14—the first case to be taken under the Act—a job advertisement came before the Equality Tribunal. The respondent had advertised for a '*young and dynamic professional*' and further that '*the ideal candidate will be young, dynamic*'. The complainant argued that such wording indicated an intention to discriminate. The phrase 'young' connotes young in years and not middle age or old, it was argued. The respondent contended that the term 'young and dynamic' was not age-related criteria, but rather that 'young' and 'old' were vague concepts.

The Equality Officer found that the term *young* did constitute a breach of s 10 of the Act and was discriminatory on the age ground. It should be noted that in such a case, both the advertiser and the publisher may be found guilty of these offences. In contraventions of this nature, maximum fines may be imposed.

Post-qualification experience has also proved problematic in respect of the Act and the possibility that such requirements are discriminatory on the age ground. In a 2004 case before the Equality Tribunal, *Noonan v Accountancy Connections* DEC-

E2004-042, discrimination on the age ground was alleged based on post-qualification experience stipulated in a job advertisement. Two senior posts were advertised, stating that the minimum experience required was '*2–3 years*'. The claimant applied for both and was informed by the respondent that he was too senior for the posts and that the company was '*pitching the roles at recently qualified candidates with two years' experience*'. The complainant contended that the experience requirement excluded all those over the age of thirty and as such he had been discriminated against on the age ground. He had twenty years' post-qualification experience. The respondent argued that the reference to being 'too senior' was not age-related, but referred to the fact that he was over-qualified for the role.

The requirement to have two years' experience applied to all prospective candidates and operated to the disadvantage of the complainant, who was in the over-thirty age group, as compared with those under the age of thirty and therefore could be complied with by a substantially smaller proportion of prospective employees in the over-thirty age group. The complainant had therefore established a prima facie case of indirect discrimination. Could the requirement be justified as being reasonable in all the circumstances?

The Equality Officer was not satisfied that the experience requirement had any specific connection with the post, particularly as it was accepted by the respondent that someone with more than two years' experience, as stipulated, would be capable of doing the job. The Equality Officer found that the respondent had not directly discriminated against the complainant, but had indirectly discriminated against him. The complainant was awarded €10,000 for distress and breach of the Act. The respondent was also ordered to draft an Equality Policy and to bring it to the attention of all relevant parties, including clients.

Focusing on the skillset required for a post advertised rather than years of post-qualification experience may prevent prospective employers from falling foul of the Act.

Interview Questions
Employers need to ensure that questions put to candidates at interview are not discriminatory on any of the nine grounds listed above. Questions to a female candidate on the number of children she has, arrangements for getting them to school, childcare arrangements, how she would look after her husband, her children and the home have all been found to be discriminatory. Where a job involves travel abroad or long hours, it may be necessary to ascertain if personal circumstances will impact on performance. In such cases questions should be asked of all candidates without reference to their personal circumstances.

Exemptions

The prohibition on discrimination is not absolute and so is subject to a number of exemptions. An employer is not obliged to employ a person who will not undertake the duties involved or is not fully competent or capable of doing the job. It should be noted, as discussed above, that a person with a disability is fully competent and capable if that person would be so upon reasonable accommodation being provided by the employer.

Requirements in relation to educational, technical and professional qualifications are allowed under the Act. Requirements as to residency, citizenship or proficiency in the Irish language are permitted in certain posts in the public sector. Discrimination on age or disability grounds may be permitted in certain sectors, e.g. the Defence Forces, An Garda Síochána and the prison service, where it can be shown that the occupational qualification is objective and proportionate. Positive discrimination is permitted where it promotes equal opportunities. Special arrangements may also be made, for example for women in relation to pregnancy or maternity issues. Positive discrimination to further the integration into the workforce of persons with disability and members of the Traveller community is allowed. Certain religious, educational and medical institutions may give more favourable treatment on the grounds of religion to an employee or prospective employee where the purpose is to maintain the religious ethos of the institution. Such institutions may also take action to prevent employees or prospective employees from undermining the religious ethos of the institution.

INDEX